How to Buy a Condominium

Also by Patricia Brooks and Lester Brooks
HOW TO BUY PROPERTY ABROAD

How to Buy
a Condominium

*Patricia Brooks
and Lester Brooks*

STEIN AND DAY/*Publishers*/New York

First published in 1975
Copyright © 1975 by Lester Brooks and Patricia Brooks
All rights reserved
Designed by Ed Kaplin
Printed in the United States of America
Stein and Day/*Publishers*/Scarborough House,
Briarcliff Manor, N.Y. 10510

Library of Congress Cataloging in Publication Data

Brooks, Lester.
    How to buy a condominium.

    1.   Condominium (Housing)—United States. I.   Brooks,
Patricia K., 1926-   joint author.   II.   Title.
HD7287.67.U5B76   643   74-28034
ISBN 0-8128-1768-0

ACKNOWLEDGMENTS

The authors wish to acknowledge with thanks the assistance of the following in supplying information and/or reviewing MSS.: Louis Squitieri, C.P.A.; David B. Wolfe, President, Community Management Corporation; Norman Jurgens, Chief Underwriter, Des Moines Office; Department of Housing & Urban Development; The Urban Land Institute, Washington, D.C., for permission to use data from *Townhouses and Condominiums: Residents' Likes and Dislikes*, Special Report (1973) by Dr. Carl Norcross.

Contents

5. En Garde!   *70*

Information sources—FHA, OILSR, SEC, FTC ...
Prospectus ... Zoning authorities, tax assessor, state
real estate commission, your banker, D&B, the people
probe ... The walkabout—what to look for ... Questioning the salesman ... Reading between the lines
and measuring the model.

6. Money Questions   *95*

Buy or rent? How to decide ... Can you afford it?
How to tell ... Closing costs, examples ... Title insurance ... Financing—VA, FHA, conventional,
private mortgage insurance ... Shopping for
financing.

7. Resort/Vacation Condominiums   *110*

What they offer, what they deliver; recreation facilities ... The project ... The prospectus ... Management ... Rental income, tax benefits, depreciation
... Examples.

8. Resales: Bargain Condominiums?   *124*

Advantages—solid cost data, problems overcome,
value higher ... Disadvantages—joining the family;
getting the facts and the documentation.

9. Condominium Fundamentals   *131*

Public offering statement ... Contract or purchase
agreement, including description, price, deposit and
escrow, title, voting power, cancellation rights,
conveying title ... Declaration or master deed
—private, limited, and common elements, owner no-
nos, recreation and other facilities, leases, costs/ex-
penses, homeowners' association (HOA), restrictions

on owners, phase construction ... Budget—annual
and monthly charges, low-balling; examples ... Survey and plans—cubes of title, "as-built" drawings,
layouts, and elevations ... By-laws—constitution of
the condomocracy; owner self-government, developer
phase-out, vetos, leases, warranties, three Rs, HOA
powers, owner responsibilities, fees and assessments,
standards of service, reserves, insurance, amendments
... Board and committees—who does what; handbook
... Management agreement—duties and responsibilities of the manager.

How to Buy
a *Condominium*

Introduction

"We live in a different era," boomed Ogilvy Pendthorpe III (the name is fictitious; the character is not) as he screwed a Virginia Slim into his gold cigarette holder and lit it. Swinging his feet from the Bokhara carpet to the surface of his massive walnut desk, the dean of American real estate advertising recalled how things had been when he had started out a generation ago.

"You're too young to remember, but we sold the potato patches of Long Island to thousands of home-hungry GIs." He gestured toward a huge aerial photo of rows of houses stretching off into infinity. "'Your own home for less than fifteen thousand dollars.' Today you can't begin to build a decent single-family house for twice that. That's why the single-family home developments are a thing of the past."

He motioned to another wall with a large aerial photo of rows and rows of two-story, attached buildings laid out in grid patterns.

"That's the new bonanza," he chortled, flicking ashes into a vast Murano ash tray. "Fifteen hundred and twenty units on two hundred acres—a forty-eight-million-dollar layout. That's the wave of the future . . . millions to be made by smart young people in condominium developments." There was a starry look in his eyes as he gazed out and beyond.

The two photos looked nearly identical to us, except that in the older one the houses were separate; in the second one they were attached.

"What?" he exclaimed. "You don't see the difference? But those are *houses;* these are *townhouses*—condominiums—all the difference in the world. Of course, there are also those. . . ." He stabbed at a large photo of high-rise buildings that looked like the Manhattan skyline with sand. "That's the Florida condominium scene. Picture eight thousand units on sixteen acres at eighteen thousand dollars plus per unit—a neat hundred-and-fifty-million-dollar package. They look like garden apartments to you? Well, my dears, we must educate you." He sighed.

So began our crash course in condominiums. Months later, after research that included going over the available information with government, academic, and real estate experts and with condominium dwellers and observers, both happies and haters, we brought together the material in this book.

This book is about condominiums. It is written for people considering buying one. In this book we deal with new residential and resort condominiums and condominium resales. We do not discuss condominium conversions.

We ruled out the entire conversion picture for two reasons: First, as Albert C. Hanna, vice-president of U.S. Steel's mortgage-banking subsidiary, puts it, "Conversions generally are a sophisticated form of abandonment. An [apartment] owner is no longer able to operate a building successfully, so he passes the problems along to the buyer." There is no way in our limited space to go into the limitless problems in renovation and conversion of an old building. Second, conversions are frequently inextricably concerned with the gritty if not inhumane forcing of tenants to buy their apartments or be evicted. In such high-pressure circumstances a book such as this can be of little help.

We have also omitted condominiums outside the United States, a subject we covered in a previous book (*How to Buy Property Abroad*). The fundamental approaches and basic principles outlined in *How to Buy a Condominium* apply in a general way to foreign condominiums as well. Caution, precautions, and careful inspection are even more important abroad than at home. And don't be carried away by the romantic ambiance of the locale. Buying in Canada is most similar to buying in the United States in terms of real estate practices and laws. Perhaps most remote from U.S. patterns is Mexico, where you may purchase only through a thirty-year trust arrangement in most desirable areas. Rules, regulations, and practices vary so from country to country in the Caribbean and Europe that it is impossible within the scope of this book to lay down hard and fast guidelines for overseas condominium purchases. Major differences from U.S.: laws, procedures, difficulty of securing reliable information (you'll find no shortage of extravagant claims), and scarcity of favorable financing. You absolutely *must* have an experienced lawyer helping you in foreign purchases. Don't, for heaven's sake, buy sight unseen from a glossy sales brochure or glib salesman. And don't snap up bargains offered by foreign taxi drivers, waiters, or other eager amateur sellers of property. Buy their souvenirs, not their condominiums.

What we attempt here is to bring together information to aid your effort to evaluate condominiums. Don't look for ratings or endorsements of specific developments. We don't offer any because condominiums are being built at the rate of 230,000 units per year—far too many to keep up with. We hope the book will give you the tools to rate them yourself.

The several condominiums we have mentioned in the text are cited for illustrative purposes only, and no endorsement is intended of any of them. For the record, we have no connection of any kind with any organization in the real estate, financial, or construction industries. We have received no favors, material assistance, or advantages explicit or implied from any individual or private organization in the preparation of this book. We have called on government and real estate officials for information and review of portions of the manuscript for factual accuracy. But we take responsibility for content.

As this is written, the greatest void in the condominium field is strong, protective federal laws to prevent the vicious rip-offs that occur in this industry. As long as federal protection is lacking, strengthening state laws is vitally important. The new Virginia "second-generation" condominium law is a model and should influence other states.

There are many signs of positive growth in the burgeoning condominium field. There are now professional condominium management companies with experience and expertise in the field. And there are the beginnings of regional condominium homeowners' associations [1] to press for legislation and consumer needs. The kernel of a condominium consumer movement is a-growing. Considering the explosive expansion of this housing phenomenon, it's high time.

Ogilvy Pendthorpe III hasn't seen the manuscript of this book. He won't like it much. It brings up too many sticky questions that require honest answers. Questions always slow down sales—sometimes even kill them—and Pendthorpe is fiercely against anything that affects sales adversely. So, though he started us off on this project, the results are almost diametrically opposite what he expected. This is a handbook for consumers, not for real estate moguls.

PATRICIA BROOKS
LESTER BROOKS

New Canaan,Connecticut

---

[1] Such as Condominium Owners Association, 166 N.E. 4th, Miami, Fla.; Condominium Executives Council of Florida, Inc., 5050 Biscayne Boulevard, Miami, Fla.; Council of Condominiums of New York State, 412–21 No. Broadway, Yonkers, N.Y. Also the fledgling National Association of Condominium Owners, National Press Building, Washington, D.C.

1

Condomania, Condominiums, and You

> No man but feels more of a man in the world if he
> have a bit of ground that he can call his own.
> However small it is on the surface, it is four thou-
> sand miles deep; and that is a very handsome
> property.
>
> —CHARLES DUDLEY WARNER

What is a condominium?

Contrary to rumor, it is *not* an international oil cartel.

Nor is it, in spite of your uncle Louie's insistence, an ancient Roman birth-control device.

It is a legal arrangement whereby you can own outright an apartment, semiattached house, townhouse, or free-standing house in a multiple-unit development. You hold a recordable deed free and clear, and may lease, sell, bequeath, modify, furnish, and occupy the premises independent of other unit owners.

In addition, you own a portion of the facilities and "common areas." These may include streets, walks, parking spaces, gardens, beaches, yards, and surrounding land, plus swimming pool or tennis courts and all jointly held recreational facilities, plus essential features such as the roof, elevators, hallways, heating plant, outdoor lighting, and other necessary elements.

You won't find a bronze plaque showing that you own the

rose garden or fifty square feet of the roof, however. These common areas are owned by all unit owners in "undivided interests." That means that you all own these features together and no owner has any right to exclude the others from access to or enjoyment of them.

Condominiums have distinct advantages. Your deed makes you an individual owner of an individual unit in the development. You have no responsibility for the taxes, mortgage obligations, or other debts of your neighbors. (In a cooperative apartment, when one owner defaults on a payment, his fellow owners must share the debts.)

Your condominium home cannot be foreclosed for other owners' debts. Your tax bill is for the taxes on your unit only. (In a cooperative apartment, there is one tax bill for the entire development and each owner pays his proportionate share. If one does not pay, his fellow owners must pay his share in addition to their own or face the prospect of legal action and ultimate tax sale of the entire building.) You will have to pay your share of taxes on the condominium's common areas and facilities, however. You also will be billed for your share of maintenance and upkeep costs, reserves, and the expenses of management and insurance. Your share is determined on a proportionate basis, at cost.

You, as an owner, are automatically a member of the condominium association, which elects a board of directors to run the development. If the development is large and/or complex, the board may hire a professional manager or management company. This is the element that makes for so-called carefree or maintenance-free living. Sharing the costs of upkeep, painting, repairs, sewage, trash disposal, lawn-keeping, snow and leaf removal, gardening, equipment care, and supervision of recreation facilities makes condominium living economical and attractive to millions.

Much confusion stems from the fact that a condominium is a form of ownership, not a type of building. Any architectural style, shape, or size can be a condominium, whether it's Aristotle Onassis' Olympic Tower office and luxury residence building on New York's Fifth Avenue, President Ford's resort ski lodge at Vail, Colorado, or your aunt Millie's retirement unit in Leisure Village, U.S.A.

Moral: You can't tell a condominium by its cover. But you can tell one by its deed. It is the deed that is the essence of condominium ownership. And it is the deed that makes condominiums so attractive to so many Americans in search of low-, moderate-, and even high-priced new housing. For thousands of Americans condominiums fulfill the dream of "a home of our own."

This is a revolutionary change from a generation ago. In post–World War II America, everyone (or so it seemed) dreamed of having a house of his own with a bit of land out in the country "away from it all." Like Mr. Blandings.

Remember Mr. Blandings? J. Holocoup Blandings?

Cary Grant played him in the movie *Mr. Blandings Builds His Dream House* in the late 1940s. The story was about the couple who found an 1890s farmhouse nestled into a hillside on fifty country acres near New York City. They fell in love with the place, bought it for $11,500. It was a bargain, they thought, for three bedrooms, a huge dining room, and a country fireplace in a beamed living room. The only problem with this beautiful white clapboard bargain was that it was uninhabitable.

The bittersweet humor of the Blandingses' story was their experience in putting "a few extra dollars" into making it "livable." Besides their pungent encounters with well-diggers, stonemasons, carpenters, and contractors, the Blandingses had their problems with money. In the end, Blandings added up his expenses to "put the place in shape" and discovered that his total investment was $56,263.97, five times what he had expected.

Today Blandings' land alone would be worth more than half a million dollars. His converted, restored, reconstructed house would bring $100,000 or more. The average price of a new house was $24,700 in January 1972. At the end of 1974—twenty-four months later—the average was 50 percent more: $37,100. The American Bankers Association reports that in the past ten years, 1964–1974, the price of the land on which a house is built has increased at an annual rate of 9.1 percent. Furthermore, the average size of building lots has *shrunk* from 8,202 to 6,990 square feet. The net effect has been an average hike in land costs of 13.5 percent each year since 1967. Housing prices have been ticking upward at the rate of 12 to 15 percent per year.

So the Blandings story seems quaint in today's inflated housing market. If Blandings' son wanted to build his own dream house today, four Ls would mitigate against it. The prices of land, labor, loans (meaning interest rates), and lumber (meaning building materials) have driven out of sight the cost of building a single-family house. Professor Karl Pearson, head of real estate education at the University of Michigan, predicts that "the single-family house, to some degree, will become a luxury only for the affluent." The general inflationary spiral has also narrowed housing options available to almost any but high-income families.

But that doesn't mean that Blandings, Jr., and the rest of us have to take to caves. If single-family housing construction is heading, dodo-fashion, toward extinction, as some experts believe, and if raw land selling for as much as $10,000 (and more) per acre makes build-it-ourselves too expensive, where do we go from here?

Into condominiums, that's where.

You can see this trend for yourself. In any community where land is scarce and is selling at premium prices, chances are that sizable chunks of it are being snapped up by eager speculators and developers and turned into condominium projects. It's a case of supply and demand. The demand for middle-class housing has outstripped the supply of reasonably priced one-family housing in populated areas. To fill the vacuum? *Voilà!* Condominiums!

Look at it this way. How would you like to buy a three-bedroom home with a swimming pool, tennis courts, and all maintenance taken care of for between $20,000 and $50,000? Where? Right in Suburbia, U.S.A. In a condominium.

In these post-Blandings days, you'll be lucky to find a three-bedroom, thirty-year-old ranchhouse on a quarter acre in an outlying suburb within an hour's commute from a major city for $60,000. But for less than that you should find a selection of comfortable, new three-bedroom townhouses with private terraces, well landscaped, with swimming pool, private clubhouse, and tennis courts, and with all outdoor chores such as lawn-mowing, snow-shoveling, and exterior upkeep handled for you—in a condominium.

There's no way you can match these values in your standard, one-family private housing for the same money. The exact dollar figures vary in different parts of the United States, but in each instance condominiums show savings of 10 to 44 percent over the cost of conventional housing. Such economy is a considerable attraction, of course, to would-be homeowners. Condominiums have considerable attractions for other people also. These attractions account for their popularity in these times of hard-pressed paychecks. Let's take a look at some of them.

A condominium is several things at the same time, depending on who is looking at it. For prospective homeowners who can't afford to build their own houses, for those who want the equity of homeownership but wish to escape the drudgery of house and yard maintenance, and for those who want the tennis, pool, golf, or other recreational amenities that they could never afford on their own, a condominium may be the answer. Without question it gives its residents the psychological, physical, and financial benefits that accompany homeownership.

For a town, a condominium is something else again. Condominium owners provide far more stability than renters. As homeowners, condominium owners tend to participate in community affairs. And condominiums pay more in taxes than apartments. They require similar if not equal town services —usually a net gain in tax revenue for the community. Here's how it works, as described by Dr. George Sternlieb, director of the Center for Urban Policy Research at Rutgers University:

> If a two-bedroom garden apartment is built as a rental unit, the municipality has to assess it on the basis of construction cost—say $16,000—or rental income.
>
> Let's say it rents for $225 a month. If the builder wants to sell his rental project, he can get about seven times the annual rent—$18,900 a unit.
>
> But if the project is built as a condominium, the town can assess it on the basis of the sale price of each unit. This could range from $22,000 to $24,000. So the town could easily realize an additional 16% or more in taxes from the condominiums.

For the real estate developer/builder, a condominium has still other advantages. It is, as one expert puts it, purely and simply a "money machine." Take the above-mentioned two-bedroom garden apartment. A builder could make a profit selling these at $18,900 per unit. Obviously, he's going to make more profit selling to condominium buyers at $22,000. Furthermore, selling the property this way spares the builder the responsibility of a long-term mortgage and the headaches of being a landlord. The condominium profit arrives immediately, as soon as the units are sold, rather than being spread over a period of years in the form of rental income.

Another factor of importance: A condominium generally is easier for a builder to finance than is a rental property. Here's an example worked up in mid-1974 by an expert, Thomas E. Brewton of the nation's largest mortgage brokerage house, Sonnenblick-Goldman Corporation of New York:

Take a 220-unit garden apartment project in the New York metropolitan area suburbs—Westchester or Bergen

County, for instance—with monthly rents averaging $228. The total annual rent would be $601,920.

With average expenses and vacancies, the appraised value of this project would be about $4 million. On that amount the maximum permanent mortgage available—roughly 75 percent of the appraised value—would be $3 million.

This $3 million ceiling on the mortgage would mean that the construction loan—money borrowed by the developer to pay costs until the project is completed—would also be limited to $3 million top. Yet this would cover only 80 to 85 percent of the builder's total costs. That, it need scarcely be said, means that somebody has to come up with the scratch: $530,000 to $750,000. And in tight-money times, that's not easy.

Now if the same project were developed as a condominium rather than as a rental complex, the units would be priced to sell for an average price of $28,500, a price very competitive with the single-family home market in New York's suburbs. (Yes, there is a discrepancy on price. Professor Sternlieb estimates market price at a conservative $22,000; Brewton, the mortgage professional, estimates the market price at an average of $28,500. That's the real estate biz for you.)

As a condominium the project's appraised value would be its sellout price—the sum of all the unit prices—or 220 × $28,500 = $6,270,000. The construction loan for the project *could* be as high as 80 percent of the sellout price—$5,016,000 [1] (fully 67 percent greater than the rental project). This would probably cover all development costs, even allowing additional expenses for a condominium's elaborate recreational facilities and an intensive sales campaign.

If you were the developer, which would you build—the rental apartment project or the condominiums? It shouldn't be too difficult a choice—after all, the condominiums can be

---

[1] In a tight money market it would probably be difficult to get this much.

built with the lender's money, not yours. And if you were given the option of owning a project with an appraised value of $4 million or one valued at $6,270,000, which way would you jump?

Precisely! Which helps explain why condominiums have become so popular with builder/developers. Many of them say (and they're putting their money where their mouths are) that the wave of the future in U.S. homeownership is condominiums.

O.K., if condominiums are so great, where have they been all your life? Relative late arrivals on the U.S. housing scene, condominiums have a long history elsewhere. The concept goes back even further than early Roman times. The earliest known reference is in Babylonian documents of 2000 B.C. which recount the sale of a first floor of a house with the owner retaining title to the second floor.

Papyrus #4721891 in the Brooklyn Museum is a condominium deed, written in 434 B.C., which describes an apartment, its boundaries, and specific instructions about the right of sale, and includes title insurance. Only the by-laws governing the management of the building and regulations about common elements are not specified. Otherwise it could have been written today as a passable condominium deed.

During Roman times and then later in the Middle Ages, condominiums were a way of dealing with the city problems of population growth and land scarcity. When the walled cities of medieval Europe burst their seams and the urban populations began to spill out into the surrounding countryside, need for condominiums declined.

Early in this century there was another condominium upsurge. Spain, Belgium, Germany, and Great Britain saw the need for expanded housing facilities, felt the pinch of land shortages, and passed condominium laws. The same thing happened in many Latin American countries, where condominiums are called "horizontal properties."

Puerto Rico was the pioneer of this type of homeownership in the United States. The island was a pressure cooker of population growth and land scarcity—the classic housing dilemma. A condominium law was passed and an island building boom began. Ten years later the United States Congress, in an amendment to the National Housing Act, extended government insurance of mortgages to cover condominiums. In 1962 the Federal Housing Authority (FHA) drew up a condominium statute based on the Puerto Rican prototype. By 1967 all fifty states had enacted legislation to permit condominium construction and ownership, but it wasn't until 1971 that the condominium impact was felt across the countryside. Even then, the mention of the word was greeted by most people with "A what?" or "Minimum which?"

In 1970 there were not quite 300,000 condominiums in the entire United States. By mid-1974 there were more than 2,000,000. In fact, 25 percent of all for-sale new housing in 1974 consisted of condominiums.

Who buys them? The real question may be not who is buying but who isn't?

In 1973 in the twenty-five major metropolitan areas one half of all new housing units built for sale were condominiums. And in 1974 one half of *all* housing sold in the entire United States was condominiums.

Part of the early condominium mythology was that this housing was for "the newlywed and the nearly dead." But recent statistics show that not only young people and retired elderly people are buying this form of housing.

Young families are frequently attracted to condominium living because of the extras as well as the sense of community, companionship for their young children, and the all-important mortgage money possibilities. In this era of inflation and a tight mortgage market, young families often lack the savings or equity for a large down payment on a house. Condominium financing is sometimes easier to come by. Some developers require less than 10 percent down payment. Many permit would-be buyers to rent the unit and apply a portion of the rental payment toward the purchase price. A few even sign agreements to repurchase the unit from the buyer at the end of a specified time period (thirty months in some cases) at the original purchase price. The inference, of course, is that the real market price will have escalated in that time and the property will be a cinch to resell.

So who else buys condominiums? Besides the young, the old, and the affluent, there are the in-betweens. ZPG (zero population growth) families, liberated singles and mingles (or unattached couples, as they are sometimes called), the divorced or widowed, all are candidates for condominium living. Many want the security, companionship, and ambiance of congenial adult condominium communities. They also want the equity of homeownership—but not the obligations and problems of a shuttered saltbox in the suburbs, with the maintenance and isolation it represents. One major nation-wide builder reports that 30 percent of his condominium buyers in the New York metropolitan area are single persons. In California's beach townhouse communities the ratio is al-most 40 percent.

The reasons why people buy condominiums vary from region to region. In the Washington, D.C., area a recent study by the Urban Land Institute, or ULI,[1] indicated that eco-nomics are of primary importance. It's no wonder, for there is an acute housing crunch in that area. Buyers want equity and say they're tired of throwing money away in rent.

A dental hygienist in the D.C. region put it succinctly in the ULI study: "For the first time I'm able to put my money into a home investment instead of rent, and it gives me a tax break. I've been here only three weeks, but already my unit is selling for two thousand dollars more than I paid. That ap-preciation is most exciting."

In California, where the climate makes yardwork almost a

[1] Carl Norcross, *Townhouses and Condominiums* (Washington, D.C.: Urban Land Institute, 1973).

year-round responsibility, 67 percent of the condominium owners surveyed had bought their townhouses primarily for freedom from maintenance chores. For them, the economic reasons were secondary. As a California schoolteacher with three children stated in the ULI study, "For four years my children and I lived in our single-family home, but the problems were too great. For a divorcee with children a townhouse is ideal. Maintenance is simple."

Easterners said that what they most enjoyed about condominium life was the relative freedom from chores—even though they bought primarily for economic reasons.

Of the 1,700 townhouse owners surveyed, 75 percent reported that they enjoy this new way of life. Many are enthusiastic. Why? They enjoy the close neighbors, the conveniences, nearby recreation, minimum maintenance required, dollar advantages over renting, and the savings over the cost of a single-family house.

There is still another type of condominium purchaser who buys a different type of condominium: the vacation-home buyer who sees in a second home an investment opportunity. Disenchantment with a long bear market in stocks has made real estate an attractive investment alternative to such buyers. Renting your unit when you're not using it is like having your cake and skiing, swimming, or golfing on it, too. (Resort/vacation condominiums are discussed in Chapter 7.)

The condominium phenomenon—resort and residential—is expanding rapidly. We hope in the following pages to provide guidelines for selecting the right condominium for your particular needs, and to forewarn you about the possible rip-offs and pitfalls lying in wait.

In short, we hope to help you avoid the mistakes that have caused unhappiness to some condominium owners in the past and to help you make the successful choices that can provide the pleasure this form of housing gives thousands of Americans.

Choosing the right condominium is not just a simple matter of "Eeny, meeny, miney, mook; I'll buy the one with the Georgian look." Beauty in condominiums is a lot more than facade deep. The time to pause, consider, poke behind the facade, and be sure of what you are doing is *before* you sign that sales contract. A major source of discontent is learning too late what should have been included in—or deleted from—that important document. Knowledge, judgment, experience count for more than luck, and should be factors in your decision-making. The next chapters will, we hope, provide you with some practical help.

Condoland ABCs

The snail, which everywhere doth roam,
Carrying his own house still, still is at home.
—JOHN DONNE

You can't tell a condominium from conventional shelter without a scorecard—in this case, a copy of the declaration or master deed.

There simply is no outward indication of what is and is not a condominium. To set the record straight, there are three basic types:

1. Residence
2. Resort/vacation
3. Business/commercial

1. *Residential condominiums:* usually built in cities, towns, or suburbs where private housing is expensive, land is scarce and costly, and there is a desperate need for housing for people of all ages. Such condominiums might be high-rise (vertical) or low-rise (horizontal), depending on the land available, size of community, and local zoning laws. Retirement condominiums and other special types for owner occupancy are also residential.

2. *Resort or vacation condominiums:* usually located in appealing areas where climate, tourist attractions, recreational facilities, and participation sports attract people of varying ages. Obviously you're not likely to find a resort con-

dominium in the heart of Pittsburgh. But resort condominiums are found on the Atlantic and Pacific coasts, in the Caribbean, in Hawaii, in lake, bay, and river areas and mountain ski spots.

3. *Commercial condominiums:* located in business zones of city or town, are usually office or retail shop buildings sold as condominiums rather than rented by a single owner. The sales contract is that of a regular condominium in which each office or shop is owned by the purchaser. As this is a subject of narrow, specific interest, commercial condominiums are not explored in this book. (Note, though, that some commercial condominiums also include residential units.)

There is no architecture that you can specify as "a condominium." There are as many kinds of architectural treatment of condominiums as there are architects. They range from A (for A-frame) to Z (for ziggurat) in their exterior treatments. But there are basically only two types of buildings for condominiums: high-rise and low-rise. Each has its advantages and certain drawbacks.

From the buyer's standpoint, both types have the fundamental condominium advantages: outright ownership, minimal maintenance, savings on cost and upkeep, and, frequently, strong "amenities packages," as the developers say.

Such packages refer to the features that attract buyers, the features over and above mere shelter. These generally are the recreation facilities such as swimming pools, tennis, squash, and paddle tennis courts, beach and boating facilities, golf, recreation halls and clubhouses, gymnasiums, and hobby or craft shops.

You'll find that both high-rise and low-rise condominiums have one or more of these amenities. As the cost of the condominium goes up, the luxury of the unit and the lavishness of the recreation facilities offered increase. Some advertise everything from card rooms to cabanas, stables and bridle paths, jogging trails, racket clubs, saunas, and Jacuzzi pools. So elaborate are some of the recreation amenities offerings that you may have trouble telling whether the condominium is a residence or a resort—until you look at the master deed and by-laws.

Comparing and contrasting the features of the high- and low-rise condominium buildings gives us this picture of the two basic types:

1. *High-rise condominiums* are buildings beyond four stories in height. They are essentially tall apartment buildings in which each apartment is owned by its occupant rather than by one landlord who owns the entire building. (You may be aware that there has recently been a rush to convert conventional apartment buildings into condominiums, selling the individual units to present tenants or others who may buy them outright. As we indicated in the introduction, we do not include such conversions in this book because they require investigation and inspection by experts if disaster is to be avoided.)

ADVANTAGES of the high-rise condominium are all those of the conventional apartment building, plus, of course, the equity of ownership and "amenities packages" not found in many rental apartment houses. In a high-rise condominium the owner has almost no maintenance or upkeep responsibilities. He may enjoy a private balcony, a pleasant view, the convenience of public transportation, and the right-at-your-elbow convenience of the compact apartment building way of life. In many high-rise condominiums the level of security can be high as well, particularly in those buildings that use closed-circuit TV in entranceways and elevators, and those that maintain around-the-clock guard/doorman service.

A unit in one of these high-rise beehives can often be less expensive than a unit of similar size in a low-rise condominium or a single-family house. This is made possible by construction economies. It can be far cheaper to build a stack of fifty housing units vertically than to string them out horizontally—especially with the rarefied prices on land these days. Density—number of units per acre—is usually much greater in high-rise than in low-rise developments. This usually means a plethora of shops, stores, and service establishments nearby, as well as convenient public transportation.

High-rise units *can* be cheaper; but they can be fabulously expensive. We know of one penthouse with a $350,000 price tag (sold in 1974) and several at the quarter-million-dollar level. Even the middle-floor units in luxury towers can be extremely dear, especially in such choice locations as Waikiki. It isn't just beach fronts that command royal prices. The most famous—or infamous—high-rise condominium of all is located in a prime spot on the Potomac, a stone's throw from the new Kennedy Center, in the heart of the nation's capital, where land is at a premium. It's no wonder that the tariffs at the Watergate are high.

DISADVANTAGES: The high-rise condominium owner faces the usual problems of all high-rise building occupants. There are the occasional hassles with lack of power, heat, water, elevator service, cleaning, maintenance, and sundry others. These are the hazards of tower living. In addition, there is always the possibility of a strike that may shut down services.

Other relatively minor problems reported by high-rise unit owners are lack of storage space—both for household goods and for cars—and lack of greenery surrounding the building. This is inevitable in areas where land costs are high and utilized to the fullest for the building itself.

2. *Low-rise condominiums* are buildings from one to four stories in height. From that point of relative certainty the rest of the definition becomes hazy. That's because you will find duplexes, fourplexes, attached, detached, semiattached, row houses, townhouses, patio homes, side-by-sides, and up-and-downs among the variety of low-rise developments.

ADVANTAGES: It's not invariably the case, but low-rise developments usually have lower density than the high-rise towers. They are likely to have grounds around the buildings.

The best of them feature green-belt areas—wooded land kept in its natural state or tidied up as a park, or plantings of shrubs, flowers, and trees which give a feeling of spaciousness to the development. Often there are patios and enclosed gardens, planned alcoves and nooks that provide privacy to the individual units.

DISADVANTAGES: Generally the low-rise condominium units require some upkeep on the part of their owners. The "limited common elements," such as shutters, doors, and patio fences, are the responsibility of the owner to whose unit they are attached. Also, he may be called upon to care for the yard, plantings, walk, and parking space that serve his unit. There may also be the screens and storm windows to put up and take down and keep painted.

Public transportation is often a problem from low-rise condominium developments, especially the smaller ones. Bus services go where the population is, and if the development does not have enough bus users to warrant service, then there may be little or none. Likewise, if its population is insufficient to warrant shops, stores, and service establishments, there may not be any nearby. The chances are, therefore, that low-rise development residents may be more dependent on auto transport than their high-rise development counterparts.

One of the most popular low-rise development styles at this time seems to be the townhouse. (While condominiums can be townhouses, not all townhouses are necessarily condominiums.) A traditional housing concept, the townhouse is well adapted to condominium uses. Each unit has a front and back yard, but shares a wall on either side with its neighbor units in a row of two or more. In the old days, townhouses were known as "row houses." Often designed to look like a group of housing units built at different times and in different styles, with different materials, some townhouses strive to simulate a block lifted bodily from Olde London Towne, complete with bow windows and dormers on one, stucco and timber on the next, brick facade on the third, gambrel roof on the fourth, with some units having balconies or porches, some one story, most with two or three. The differing facades appeal to buyers. The interiors, if well planned, can be attractive and efficient. Often the living area is on the second floor, with garage and recreation room on the first and bedrooms on the third. Skylights are used for natural light, and creative touches such as cathedral ceilings and rooms two stories high enliven the designs. Patios and enclosed gardens are added touches for many townhouses.

Lest you think that townhouses are somehow second-class accommodations and a bit crowded, let us assure you that they range in price from $24,000 to $275,000. Among their advertised features you will find center halls, libraries, skylights, wood-burning fireplaces, courtyards, private decks, storage basements, screened family rooms, terraces, poolside patios, greenhouses, "flying dens," and wine cellars!

Another element worth considering when evaluating high-rise versus low-rise condominium developments is the land plan. This enormously important feature is called variously the layout or the arrangement of buildings on the landscape. Involved is the attention to nature, the environment, ecology, and the interest of people seeking a better balance between man and nature.

In the United States it seems that high-rise developments with imaginative land plans are rare. The economics of construction and real estate usually determine that the high-rise towers are built on extremely expensive land—prime urban or resort property—and the developer must build many units on the property in order to help pay for the initial expense of the land. He cannot afford, generally, to surround the tower(s) with expanses of parkland. So it is in the low-rise developments that the imaginative use of the landscape is more likely to be found. The low-rise developments are arranged in a variety of configurations, ranging from the dreadful straight rows of attached houses set on a rigid and boring grid pattern of streets to clusters, complete with parking and walks, "salted" into the topography in pleasing and diversified arrangements designed for the convenience of the owners as well as their aesthetic enrichment.

Long-time pacesetter for all imaginative land planners is Tapiola, west of Helsinki, Finland. This "garden city" was a pioneering venture in modern community design which has had profound impact on urban planners for the past twenty years. In the 650 acres of rolling hills and ponds of Tapiola, none of the residence buildings is more than a short walk from one of the bright, attractive shop complexes where groceries, pharmaceuticals, cleaning, hairdressing, and other essential goods and services are available.

Furthermore, from their buildings, Tapiola's 17,000 residents need never cross a street or highway to the shopping complex or recreation areas—the tennis courts, gardens, and ponds where children and their elders play safely and happily. Parking and bus services are clustered. There are enough commuters to Helsinki to warrant extensive and efficient bus services. Concern both for the land and for those living in the community are evident throughout Tapiola and make it noteworthy among developments.

"What makes Tapiola successful is the idea—the land plan," says the general manager. "The important thing here is the layout, the way different types of buildings relate to each other. It is the way they are arranged, and the spaces between, that makes for a good environment."

The land plan of a condominium project—the buildings, spaces, natural features, roads, and streets—will be the major force affecting the quality of environment for generations of residents. Because the land plan is so important, the best imagination and creativity available should be invested in it. Unfortunately, if the developer is a corner-cutter, this doesn't always happen.

There are, however, many outstanding examples of this principle. One of the most imaginative ones may be Birchwood at Blue Ridge, in the town of Brookhaven, New York.

This clustered development will ultimately contain 866 homes on a 400-acre site. Fifty acres are to be town property —donated by the developer for recreational uses. The 866 condominium units are to be grouped on forty acres. The rest will be golf course and clubhouse. The virtues of the arrangement are several: the town will maintain the fifty-acre recreational land, thereby relieving the unit owners of that expense. The fifty acres become open to all residents of the town, not just those in the development, so townspeople gain. The 310 acres of golf course and landscaping will create a sense of open space and airiness to the development. Town covenants will prevent further exploitation of the site.

The essence of the clustered development is that the developer is allowed to build on lots smaller than normally permitted by the town's zoning ordinances. However, the vacant land must be kept as open space and the overall density of the project must not exceed the limits in the original zoning regulations.

Builders of clustered developments have cogent economic arguments on their side. As the president of Greater American Communities, Melvin Konwiser, points out, "Larger lots [for single-family homes] require longer street frontages, and streets are expensive. Gradually, the cost of the lot has climbed to the point where it equals 25 to 30 percent of the house cost. Only 25 years ago, the lot cost was rarely more than 10 percent."

For many condominium seekers the quality of the environment is one of the major concerns. And consumerism, with its emphasis on value, has caused people to consider condominiums and compare them with traditional types of housing. Not infrequently the comparison results in the purchase of a condominium.

Surely one of the most successful projects and one considered a model by many developers and housing specialists is Heritage Village at Southbury, Connecticut. Located in the woods about twelve miles from Waterbury, a city of over

100,000, Heritage Village was conceived as a retirement community (the new term is "adult community") with age restrictions. Owners (or at least one householder) must be at least fifty years old, and there can be no children under eighteen in residence for more than six months of the year.

Because of the project's isolated site, the original concept—admirably adhered to—was to make the project as self-sustaining as possible. A large shopping arcade, conceived along the lines of Istanbul's old covered bazaar (and actually called The Bazaar), with twenty-two shops under a single roof, meets most of the needs of the residents. The Bazaar is a fascinating building—four levels, heavily timbered, with 37,000 square feet of usable space. Adjacent to it are a drugstore, supermarket, and TV repair shop. Nearby is an inn with guest rooms and additional shops. Then there are a financial building with banks and lawyers' offices and a professional building with doctors', dentists', and optometrists' offices. An on-site ambulance service is always at the ready in case a dash to the nearest hospital is required.

Social needs of the residents are met by a central hall, called the Meeting House, with music room, card rooms, gardening workshop, printing shop, and kitchen for gourmet club activities. Also on the grounds are a men's clubhouse (for billiards, games, and reading), a women's clubhouse (for teas and bridge), the Stables Studio (for art- and craftwork), and a separate activities building with a sauna, gymnasium, whirlpool baths, an auditorium, tape and record rooms, projection room, photography lab, and woodworking shop.

Conscious of its pioneer role in a state as traditional as Connecticut, Heritage Village planners gave a unified, traditional look to the entire project. They designed all buildings, even the commercial ones, in New England farm style with gray shingles and simple lines. The design appealed to contemporary tastes as well. The project fits quite snugly into the wooded terrain that surrounds it and seems to please everybody—including old-timers in nearby towns who resisted the idea of the project at the outset. Some of the three thousand Village residents—many of them retired professionals or businessmen—have become active in community affairs, making themselves a political force in local government.

Carrying rusticity a step further is a new condominium project, Plum Run, now being constructed in rural Kentucky. It makes a virtue out of nostalgia, but it is not a private preserve for senior citizens. A nineteenth-century farm community is being simulated, including such "living history" details as shops for a saddler, blacksmith, tinsmith, and potter, all of whom will function as their predecessors did over 150 years ago.

There's more than simulation planned. Each home will have a large "keeping room" with full-wall fireplace, brick hearth, and plank floors. The key word is Utopia, but Utopia 1830s style. There'll be no golf course, but "freedom to chase butterflies, walk on the grass, or build a dam on the creek," says the developer. As part of the 941-acre "return-to-Mother-Earth" development, a 350-acre produce farm and greenhouse will be operated to make the project partly self-sustaining. If residents want to work on the farm—and get paid for it—they can.

Woods, privacy, terracing, landscaping that shields a unit from full view of its neighbors and creates an illusion of seclusion are selling points in all areas where land is at a premium and high density is a problem. On the outskirts of metropolitan New York, many residential condominiums emphasize design appeal and the natural look. "Welcome to the gentle wilderness," beckons one brochure. This often translates into wood exteriors purposely finished in muted shades of gray or brown to blend with the natural surroundings. Walls sometimes consist of large expanses of glass—big picture windows or sliding glass doors—to enhance the indoor/outdoor theme. This theme is popular even in less densely populated places such as Oregon, where buyers still crave a sense of privacy.

Owner satisfaction is just one of the reasons developers strive for a "wooded wonderland" look when possible. In certain areas such spaciousness is required for local zoning board approval of the project. Environmental impact has strongly influenced local zoning boards in many communities.

Kaufman and Broad, one of the world's largest home-building firms, reports that environmental requirements of zoning boards have doubled the time needed by developers to conceive, obtain approval, and complete a condominium (using 1971 as a base). Inevitably this means that the cost of condominiums has increased. It also means that the quality of life in such projects should be better—a factor worth considering when you invest in your future home.

3

Before You Buy

"That was a narrow escape!"—said Alice, after leaving the too-small house.

—Lewis Carroll

With the expanding condominium boom, the choices available are sometimes bewildering. But before you decide you want to live in a complex swingingly modern or one rustically colonial, there are other choices and decisions facing you—more crucial at the beginning than whether your piano fits into the living room or whether the rights to the pool are spelled out in the sales contract. These decisions are important too, but they come later.

Let's begin at the beginning. You think you might want to buy a condominium but you're not sure where. How do you check out location? Obviously much depends on your specific needs. If your job requires that you live within a certain radius of a metropolitan area, then you'll want to make forays into the suburbs surrounding that metropolis. If, on the other hand, you are contemplating retirement and a home in a warm climate, then an exploratory trip to areas of possible interest is mandatory.

RED FLAG: Buying property sight unseen and area unseen are two invitations to possible disaster.

If you think that Fort Lauderdale sounds neat but haven't

seen it, first write to the Chamber of Commerce with specific questions about health facilities, climate throughout the year, cost-of-living profile, prices of housing, and other points of particular concern to you.

Once you've targeted an area, the next step is to visit it. You should try to see it at its worst as well as at its best. If possible, you might even rent in the area first, to sample it before buying. This is especially advantageous in a potential retirement area, less necessary in a suburb of a general area you already know.

Next you'll need to compile a list of basic requirements essential to your well-being in any housing you buy. And be sure to include your emotional as well as your physical well-being. Shangri-la doesn't exist, but there's no harm in trying to come as close to it as possible. Some items for your check list:

1. *Accessibility.* Is there an airport anywhere in the vicinity? Train or bus station? Is there good public transportation so you can commute to work or get around the area easily? If you're a senior citizen, retiring doesn't mean disappearing. You'll very likely want to be somewhat accessible so that family and friends can visit you. (On the other hand, *in*accessibility might be just what the doctor ordered—depending on your temperament.) How are the roads to and from your locale? Will you have any trouble in rainy or snowy weather reaching your area or town or property? How are the access roads? Are they town-maintained?

RED FLAG: If not, this could be an unwanted cost in your annual assessment.

2. *Cost of living.* When you compare food costs with those in your present community, is there an advantage? Shop the local supermarkets, clothing stores, department stores. Check out the costs of other items that make up a sizable part of your budget: auto upkeep, gasoline, fuel, electricity and water charges, medical fees, cleaning and laundry costs, dental fees,

labor and service charges, golf, ski, or other recreation fees. The Bureau of Labor Statistics of the U.S. Department of Labor publishes annual cost-of-living figures for major cities and areas in the United States. These could provide helpful guidelines if you are considering relocating. If the project you like is isolated from a major town or city, dependent on its own markets and shops, be sure to check them very carefully. Will you be paying a premium for every quart of milk or egg you buy? If so, the relatively good price of the project could, over the long term, be canceled out.

3. *Facilities and amenities:* shops, clothing, food, entertainment, recreation, public transportation, restaurants, churches, and schools. Are the schools good? That's dandy, if you have school-aged kids. If you don't, there may be high property taxes you'd rather avoid. Is the complex on or near a lake or river or bay? Are such facilities important to your physical or emotional well-being? If not, this might involve costs you'd be happier doing without. Are there movie theaters, galleries, interesting shops, and a wide range of restaurants in the vicinity? Or would you be miles away from the nearest Big Mac? And does it matter to you? In considering the amenities and attractions of an area, investigate how much of the year they can be enjoyed. If, for instance, you are looking at a resort-type area for a possible year-round home, you may be surprised to find it practically a ghost town in the off season. Touch base with the local planning agency to see if any drastic changes are on the way.

4. *People and animals.* Keep in mind—especially if you are moving from a single-family house—that you will be living with other people in closer proximity than you may ever have done before. If you are moving from an apartment, remember the differences. A condominium means ownership. You can't call the landlord to fix your broken wall switch or to get rid of the disagreeable tenants next door. If you discover after the first night or week or month that you have made a mistake and can't stand your neighbors, you can't just break your lease and

move away. What if your children have flown the nest? You may not want to stumble over kiddy cars or scooters every time you cross the walk. If you are single and looking for companionship, by all means steer clear of that super-looking Spanish hacienda complex where the inhabitants look like models out of Geritol ads. If the project is brand-new and few other owners have moved in to establish their beachheads, then simple observation won't help much. But you can ask the developer for a profile of the kind of owner to whom he's pitching the complex. Often you can absorb a feeling of the type of owner a builder is aiming to attract by his ads. Ads that stress "adult environment" are not aiming for the Pampers set.

As important as children—or the lack of them—are neighbors and friends. Size up the complex. Spend time observing and talking to the residents. You'll soon sense whether it's your kind of place. Age isn't always a factor. One senior citizen living in a condominium complex of predominantly young families says, "I wouldn't live in one of those 'old folks' homes' for anything. Life there just rotates around the three Gs—gardening, golf, and guzzling. I keep young by contact with all these young neighbors of mine."

Do the owners seem friendly? Overly so? Too kaffee-klatchish for your tendency to solitude? A condominium is not a single-family house where you can burrow in and live like a hermit if you choose. A frequent complaint of disgruntled condominium owners is noisy neighbors. It is possible in a condominium to maintain some isolation from the neighbors, but not all the time. There are meetings of the homeowners' association when community is the name of the game.

How about pets? Do you have a beloved cat or dog who whither thou goest, so goes he? Then don't sign the contract for a gorgeous Georgian townhouse and discover later, rather than sooner, that the by-laws prohibit pets. Conversely, if you can't abide anything that hops, struts, purrs, slinks, or slithers, you may find yourself in a project literally crawling with pets. One of the most frequently voiced complaints is about dogs—dogs that roam and despoil the sidewalks, gardens, and recreation areas. One retired couple complained, "Our next-door neighbors have four dogs and they all bark. At times we feel we're living inside a dog kennel." Another owner who subsequently sold his condominium told Dr. Carl Norcross, "Many people owned dogs and did not walk them, but let them run loose. Dogs tore up garbage, ruined lawns and shrubs, and were a common nuisance. Even people who walked their dogs let them do their business on the common greens. Sometimes you couldn't take a step without getting into a dog's mess."

5. *Health.* Investigate the health care available. This is probably no problem if you are settling in or near a major urban area. But rural areas can pose problems. If you or a member of your family have a special health problem, you need to be sure that up-to-date facilities and medical care are available locally to handle any problems.

6. *Safety.* Find out about fire and police protection. Are the facilities adequate for the needs? How far is the unit you're considering from a fire hydrant? Inquire about the local fire district, if its equipment is adequate or antiquated, and if it is a professional or volunteer crew. You'll want to ask similar questions about the police force. How many men cover your district, what has the local crime rate been, what trend—if any—is evident? What security does the complex itself offer? Is it over- or underprotected for its needs and numbers and the area in which it is located? (Some condominium ads stress security precautions such as "private electronic entrance gate for condominium owners," or "each unit equipped with an individually controlled electronic security system directly connected with Security Center," or "24-hour Security Center where a uniformed officer screens and announces all visitors.") If the security precautions seem overemphasized to the point of paranoia, perhaps too much of your monthly maintenance fees will be allotted to unneeded security.

7. *Local hazards.* At the top of this list are natural calami-

ties such as hurricanes, earthquakes, floods, cyclones, blizzards. Is the area you're considering in the hurricane, earthquake, or tornado belt? What about insurance covering such potential dangers? Is the general area or specific locale of the complex in a low land pocket where seasonal rains could cause flooding? How about man-made hazards such as pollution? What is the major industry of the area? Is there any danger of pollution from petrochemical plants, atomic energy plants, factories belching smoke into the air and/or waste into the waters? Check the locale carefully on this score. What is the source and supply of fresh water? Many a Bucolic Bay has turned into a potential Bubonic Bay through overbuilding, industrialization, and subsequent pollution.

Health hazards are serious business. Check out the climate at *all* seasons, zenith and nadir. If you can't stand humidity and don't like air conditioning or want to avoid the expense of a unit clicking away twenty-four hours a day, then there are certain parts of the South you should avoid. If you desire air conditioning, be sure of the reliability of the local electric power—and its cost.

Then there are the minor irritants. Local wildlife could drive you bonkers. Better to learn of its existence before buying into the area. If snakes are the bane of your life, check the local reptile population. One friend of ours fled an area in defeat after a year spent dodging snakes indoors and out. Cockroaches, sand gnats, mayflies, deer flies, sand fleas, mosquitoes, and other nuisances might make life unbearable. Or they might not deter you from buying, but might lead you to consider renting out your unit during the buggy season.

You might think of other critical items to add to your shopping list. Once you've targeted your area and zeroed in on it, you'll want to look at all the projects your shoe leather can endure before John Hancock time.

If you are buying with the thought of eventual resale, you'll want to approach the purchase with some specific objectives in mind. Researchers have found, from numerous surveys, that certain key elements have much greater sales appeal than others. They will also add to your enjoyment of your condominium home while you're living in it.

Points to consider:

1. *Quality of workmanship.* Don't settle for cut corners on construction or materials. Condominium owners who are most satisfied tend to live in units well made with little need for repairs and few problems.

2. *Density.* The lower, the better. Fewer than seven units per acre are considered good and seem to relate directly to owner contentment. Discontent mounts when density exceeds nine units per acre.

3. *Landscaping.* Look for a complex that is well land-scaped, with shade trees and shrubs that ensure a measure of privacy. In a recent ULI survey, townhouse owners were asked to cite land-plan features of greatest appeal and importance to them, features that would be the greatest inducements to them to buy. They chose the following:

Features	*Mentioned by (%)*
Trees, woods, landscaping	42
Open space	27
Play or recreation space	17
Convenience to shops	14
Away from main roads	12
Water, lakes, streams, etc.	11
Privacy and quiet	10
Convenience to schools	9
Space around buildings	9
Convenience to facilities	8
High site, good drainage	7
Good access to main roads	6
Good design	6
Good parking	5

4. *Organization of complex.* The happiest owners are to be

found in projects arranged in loose clusters—short rows of houses with space between rows, around cul-de-sacs or circles or open squares.

5. *Location of unit.* Most desirable, according to studies, are outside locations and/or end units. Residents prefer the perimeter with its sensation of greater space, less crowding. End units often command higher prices because of the extra space and the frequently different exterior or size. Downhill townhouses are preferred (because they have a two-story front and a three-story back, the basement converts easily to a family room with a door to the garden or patio). They sell fastest and at premium prices. The uphill townhouses have garages under the second or third floor, but patios and gardens must be dug out of the hillside and the living room is up one flight from the street.

6. *Type of unit.* Experience indicates that one-story townhouses are most popular and sell first. Single-story units interspersed among two- and three-story townhouses within a complex almost invariably sell first. Units with completely enclosed patios (for greater privacy) are also popular. Other assets for resale are: large kitchens, abundant storage space, separate dining rooms, foyers or entrance halls, several bathrooms, spacious rooms, minimal stairs, family rooms, decent basements, living rooms in the rear (for privacy and a better view).

7. *Parking facilities.* Inadequate parking is one of the greatest single sources of owner discontent. The more parking space your unit has, the better—preferably more than two spaces. The formulas used by builders for parking facilities for townhouse condominiums have usually been based on apartment families. Townhouse families are larger and more affluent, and have more recreation vehicles—boats, campers, trailers—and more cars. They also, frequently, have more teenagers who own cars. And they entertain considerably more often than apartment dwellers. The net result is that two parking spaces are not enough for the family, much less guests.

Furthermore, since storage space is scarce, the garage that may be a feature of some townhouses (especially in California) usually is converted early into a lateral attic, stuffed with stored household goods and tools. Thus the cars are homeless and are parked in the driveway or street. The parking problem remains. One California condominium owner reported, "The streets are so narrow, parking is forbidden. Most families have two cars and use their garages for storage. We have to rent space outside for our boat and trailer. In the guest parking area near us there have been three cars not moved for seven months. All this makes for bad parking problems."

8. *Recreation facilities.* In spite of the condominium ads that emphasize the glorious golf course, the most popular sports facilities by far are swimming pools and tennis courts. Features cited by condominium owners as most favored are, in this order:

1. Swimming
2. Children's play areas
3. Tennis
4. Paths for walking, jogging, cycling
5. Water sports
6. Golf
7. Clubhouse activities
8. Basketball
9. Skating
10. Baseball, softball
11. Picnic and barbecue

A newsletter for developers, the *P.U.D. Review,* recently listed five major fears of potential condominium purchasers. They are:

1. Noisy neighbors
2. Association control
3. Management services
4. Assessments
5. Resale

The first four are discussed in detail in Chapter 9. The fifth question usually is "Can I sell my unit at or above the price I've paid for it?" While no one can promise an unending escalation in housing prices, the trend is certainly upward. If you buy a unit in a well-constructed and attractive condominium complex in a desirable location, this question shouldn't cause you any worries. The location of the unit, as we've just explained, is another dimension to rapid resale possibilities.

It isn't unusual for a condominium hunter with the "smarts" to stalk a dozen projects before finding the right one. In the hunting you might discover that condominium living really is not for you after all. We recall the poor owner who told Carl Norcross, "Late at night I hear my neighbor snoring. Thin walls have inhibited my sex life and feeling of privacy. I'm looking forward to building or buying my own home." The time to make such a crucial discovery is *before* you sign aboard. If you know anyone who owns a condominium, plan a visit. If possible, spend a day or two. Get a feeling of the life style and whether or not it really is for you. It may not be.

4

Condorealities: Pluses and Minuses

> My dwelling was small and I could hardly entertain
> an echo in it.
>
> —HENRY DAVID THOREAU

The first and for many the most important reason so many people buy condominiums today rather than new single-family detached houses is price. Because of the savings in the cost of land and construction, builders can offer condominiums from 10 to 44 percent less than the price for comparable single-family houses. What is more, they can and frequently do offer superior recreation facilities—swimming pools, tennis courts, beaches and marinas, shuffleboard, even golf courses on some of the expensive and elaborate developments.

If you are comparison shopping, you'll find that the rental house or apartment you're considering should be weighed against a comparable condominium whose price is approximately nine times as great as the annual rental. In other words, if the house rents for $400 per month, its annual rental is $4,800 and a comparable condominium should sell for about nine times that: $9 \times \$4,800 = \$43,200$.

Of course there are wide differences. You can save by buying a unit on a lower floor of a high-rise building. Comparable apartments generally increase in price at a rate of some 2 to 3 percent per floor as you go up. The exception, of course, is the walkup, especially above the second floor. If you're willing to climb the stairs, you may save up to 15 percent over the first-floor units. Another factor is location—a condominium unit that faces away from the sea or the mountains usually is less expensive than its sister unit that has the glorious view—sometimes as much as 25 percent less expensive.

In recent years condominiums have been profitable not only for the builders. Especially in metropolitan areas, the increase in value of condominium units has been extraordinary. In one affluent New York suburb the banker we interviewed winked knowingly when he learned we were writing about condominiums.

"Sharp investment," he said. "Mighty sharp. In the last four years we've bought and sold dozens of 'em for customers. All types. High-rise, townhouses, resort villas, even some condominiums abroad. First one we bought was for Max Seward when he retired and sold his house here in town. Bought a two-bedroom attached townhouse in Legacy Village for thirty-two-five. In six months he decided it was too small and sold it for thirty-seven thousand. Realized it was a good deal and bought three more, in addition to one to live in. He's bought and sold half a dozen since then, averaging about four thousand dollars' profit each time. Better than the stock market, he says. I'm looking at one myself, up at Harbor Acres on the Sound. After all, I'm only a year from retirement."

The capital gain from real estate sales can be substantial, as our banker friend points out. In choice areas near major cities condominium developments of high quality are in demand. Their units have enjoyed startling increases in price on the resale market. The quality of the original construction, the attention to the setting, provision of recreational facilities, and good maintenance have been key factors in their market appreciation.

The fact that yours is one of many units means that the upkeep should be less costly on the exterior and common elements than it would be if you had to handle it by yourself. In other words, the condominium management should be able to secure favorable prices on supplies, paint, everything from grass seed to saplings, and for the labor to carry out needed work—preventive and current maintenance as well as repair work.

Condominiums have a distinct advantage over cooperative apartments in that you will be able to get your own financing independently with the same freedom to bargain on size of mortgage and terms that any purchaser of a single-family house may have. Furthermore, you are liable only for your own mortgage and your own unit. If your neighbor defaults on his mortgage, it won't have any effect on your financial liability (as it might in the case of a co op). You are responsible for your taxes and yours alone. And if a lien or assessment is slapped on your neighbor, you have no obligation if he fails to pay up. This means that your neighbor's money problems need not prevent you from selling your unit whenever you wish, for his problems cannot derail your sale.

ADVANTAGES

As a condominium property owner you have certain advantages over those who rent.

1. You usually can renovate, remodel, change your condominium unit as you wish. (Exception: Cases where the condominium by-laws prevent this—resort/vacation condominiums, for example.) Not only can you usually make changes, but you will be eligible for home improvement loans to finance major projects such as a closet or bath. Tenants and those who live in cooperative apartments generally cannot secure such loans.

2. Many states have special provisions in the tax laws to benefit homeowners. These may be exemptions for veterans, the aged and infirm, widows, and homesteaders. In Florida, for instance, a homestead exemption of up to $5,000 of assessed valuation is available to legal residents, but not to tenants or absentee landlords. In Hawaii, it's $8,000.

3. As we have noted, a condominium can be a valuable hedge against inflation, whether the increase in its value

comes from inflation itself, population pressure, or other causes. You probably will be able to sell for a profit if you need to do so.

4. After your equity in the condominium has increased, whether from your mortgage payments or increases in market value, you should be able to borrow against this equity. You may refinance your mortgage at a higher figure through your bank. Whether it is a new and larger mortgage loan or simply an increase in the existing one, your condominium serves as security.

5. If you sell your home and purchase a condominium as your principal residence within one year, you will escape capital gains tax on that transaction up to the amount paid for the condominium. You can't escape any of the tax if you sell and move into a rental dwelling.

6. You have the tax benefits the Internal Revenue laws give all homeowners. In other words, your allowable deductions include (a) mortgage interest and (b) state and local real estate taxes. These can be substantial. For instance:

Cost of
condominium: $40,000
Amount of mortgage 30,000 @ 8½% interest = $2,550 per year
Real estate taxes   1,600 per year
Interest + taxes = $4,150

The benefit to you depends on your tax bracket, as follows:

	20% bracket	*30% bracket*	*40% bracket*
Interest + taxes of			
$4,150	$830	$1,245	$1,660
Saving equal to	$69.17/mo.	$103.75/mo.	$138.33/mo.

If you never considered the benefits of condominium ownership over renting in dollars and cents before, that should put a different polish on the old apple!

As we have reported, in many areas the market value of

homes, including condominiums, has moved up at alarming rates, from 12 to 20 percent per year. If your condominium does likewise, you may find that your $40,000 investment has increased in value as much as $3,400 the first year (at 8.5 percent, for example), even more the second year, and so on, as follows:

INCREASE IN VALUE
@ 8.5% PER YEAR

Original cost: $40,000

Year	Increase	Total Value
1	$ 3,400	
2	3,689	
3	4,003	
4	4,343	
5	4,712	$60,147
6	5,112	
7	5,547	
8	6,019	
9	6,530	
10	7,085	$90,440
11	7,687	
12	8,341	
13	9,050	
14	9,819	
15	10,654	$135,991

Financing, in the days of interest rates of more than 10 percent, can be an almost insurmountable barrier to the dream of owning a home. In the case of a condominium, the developer often will offer more favorable financing terms to buyers than would a bank. As an example, when this was written at the end of 1974, the giant U.S. Home Corporation was offering purchasers of its Mountain Creek Townhouses in

Dallas conventional mortgages at 8.75 percent with only 5 percent down payment required. If you could qualify for a Veterans Administration–guaranteed mortgage, the corporation would give you a 7.75 percent mortgage with no down payment and closing costs of only $1.00!

In addition to financial advantages such as these from condominium ownership, there are others worth mentioning. The recent ULI survey of townhouse owners found three-fourths of them pleased with their new way of life. Some were enthusiastic about the landscape, woods, and elbow room. Others raved about the recreational facilities. Still others were keen on the physical arrangement of the buildings and the advantages of their layout or design. And many mentioned the social situation with delight. An auditor's wife included a number of these features in her response: "Townhouse living is extremely pleasurable. We have as much space as in many fifty-thousand-dollar homes. We are in a well-planned community with play space and wooded areas. The closeness of homes creates a closer feeling among neighbors. We like the privacy of our three levels; our kids can go to bed on the top level without being disturbed by radio or TV."

The Urban Land Institute study found that the features townhouse owners liked most about their housing investments were these:

	Features	*Mentioned by (%)*
1.	Easy maintenance	61
2.	Dollar value	40
3.	Good neighbors	25
4.	Good house design, floor plan	23
5.	Recreation facilities	15
6.	Environment	13
7.	Good location	13
8.	Security	11
9.	Privacy	11

Look at the condominium ads in your newspaper. If they're like most, the ads put emphasis on five features:

1. Enjoyment of the natural beauty of the land
2. Recreational facilities and/or activities
3. Freedom from maintenance chores
4. Security
5. Community

1. *Ecology.* More and more stress seems to be placed these days by developers on preservation of existing natural beauties of an area—its trees, hills, ponds, shore, even its rocks. Some developers carefully augment nature by creating ponds and inlets, adding trees, plantings, and gardens. They know it is not only good land management to do these things but smart business as well, for people who appreciate such features are willing to pay extra for them. That means more profit and quicker sales for the builder. But after all, the developer presumably has enhanced the lives of his customers by his actions and has prevented rapacious exploitation of the countryside. He's entitled to his profit.

2. *Recreational facilities.* If condominium ads do not beckon you softly to walk barefoot among the wild flowers in the woods, they may challenge the outdoorsman or athlete in you. At the moment we are looking at condominium ads headlining swimming pools (some developments have more than one; some have indoor and outdoor pools), tennis courts, a marina and beach club, shuffleboard and croquet (for the older clientele), paddle tennis, and golf. Some unusual developments offer many of these.

You may be rich enough to own some recreational facilities outright. But if you're like most of us, your most likely access to them may be through ownership of a condominium that includes one or more of them. (In some developments recreational facilities are leased. We are talking here about condominiums that own, not lease, their facilities.) Few of us can expect to enjoy a swimming pool along with a $30,000 home otherwise. Many condominiums have lake or shore frontage from which swimming and boating are enjoyed. Others feature marinas with moorings that may be leased for an additional fee. Many of these condominiums have clubs with facilities open only to members. These often include golf clubs or beach- or pool-side clubhouses with saunas, showers, and snack facilities. Some are large and prosperous enough to have professional management and pro shops.

3. *Freedom from maintenance.* "Carefree living" is the pitch used by many condominium developers, and it is a powerful persuader. Studies of owners indicate that escape from the home upkeep chores is one of the most compelling reasons for buying a condominium. You would expect this to be a strong reason for retired people to buy, but it is a remarkably important motivator of young condominium buyers as well. In fact, in California, where the yard demands attention year round, this appears to be the single strongest motivation for buying a townhouse condominium. The ULI study found that in the West 74 percent said "freedom from maintenance" was the reason they bought. In the East the figure was 44 percent. This is particularly understandable when you know that much of California has a climate that requires watering shrubs and lawns almost daily. The necessary yardwork is time-consuming and expensive for individual homeowners —and finding reliable service is not easy.

Both freedom from maintenance and enjoyment of recreational or natural facilities are tremendous attractions. However, no one should delude himself. They are far from free. In fact, their costs sometimes lead to serious controversy among homeowners. (See "Disadvantages.")

4. *Security.* It may be professional, as in large developments that have guards on duty around the clock. It may be organizational, as in all developments large enough to have a management staff in attendance throughout the week. But in almost all cases the condominium residents constitute a community, not a faceless group of anonymous tenants.

There is security in each of these elements of community organization.

It is reassuring to know that if you are away from home for a few hours, days, or even weeks, your home is protected by the guard system, cared for by regular maintenance, and checked by the management. And perhaps instilling a degree of confidence that cannot be measured is the fact that your neighbors will watch your unit because it is to their interest as well. Anyone who has a major investment that depends substantially on the continued safety and good condition of adjacent housing units has compelling reasons in addition to friendship to keep an eye on your place.

"We are very impressed with our first townhouse," said a working couple with two children to the ULI researchers. "We have more privacy here than in any house we've owned. People are very friendly. We enjoy being able to walk around in the evenings without fear. The association keeps everything in top condition. We love it."

5. *Community.* Another condominium advantage—not stressed in the ads and sometimes misunderstood—is that of active participation in a viable, comprehensive, manageable community. We have traveled far as a nation and in our living patterns from the days when most Americans lived in small communities. In the early days of the Republic there was strength in such communities. Their strength came, in part, from the commonality of interests, the interdependence of citizens, the high degree of face-to-face interchange. Each person was known in some measure to all his fellows. And the hard-won rights of the newly independent American citizens to self-government were exercised with clear understanding of the effects of their decisions. They could not help understanding the ramifications of their actions because the results were immediate and visible for all to see and experience.

Condominiums constitute to a remarkable degree a return to this smaller community. The physical arrangement of the condominium development often makes this inevitable. The common interests of the residents make it necessary. The homeowners' association makes it mandatory.

You get a sense of this in the comments from owners such as this one, impressed by the advantages of both the physical surroundings and the social milieu: "The developer has gone to great lengths to retain natural wooded areas within the clusters," he told the ULI researchers. "These provide aesthetic pleasure and relaxation. We highly value the open, cosmopolitan social and cultural atmosphere. There are no restrictions against minority or foreign residents. People coming here know it is an integrated community and accept it as such. Thus, virtually all the racial tension which plagues other developments has been avoided."

Another resident enthusiast is more succinct and obviously delighted in his response to the ULI survey: "Due to the high density here, the quality of neighbors can make a tremendous difference. Our neighbors are young and friendly and we have much in common. For this reason our block has a fantastic community spirit that has made life here very enjoyable."

To many people the condominium living experience is an awakening: For the first time they have the experience of participating in a group that makes basic decisions that determine the quality and style of life they will lead. For thousands of people it is an exhilarating experience, especially for those whose entire lives have been spent in apartments where their leases specifically prevented them from anything but occupying the premises and paying the rent.

These escapees from passive existence find it a voyage of widening discovery as they take up questions ranging from grass cover and plantings to lighting of the grounds and use of parking and recreation facilities. How many of them realize that the questions they grapple with are akin to those our ancestors faced: What uses to be allowed of Lexington's village green? What disposition of timber cut on village property? How much to authorize for the "rude bridge" across Concord brook?

The enlistment of the energies and talent of our citizens in managing their own living environment is a phenomenon that has caught the attention of social scientists and philosophers as well as economists and marketing specialists. As a result you can expect an expanding output of analyses and projections and more and more consumer products based on the condominium way of life. The conventional wisdom is that vandalism, littering, and other socially unattractive actions against property are minimized in condominium communities because pride of ownership in the individual unit as well as the commonly owned areas is high. Furthermore, the governing rules are not handed down from an unknown, impersonal authority. They are set out by the by-laws, interpreted by the association and its board of directors. New rules are democratically arrived at and approved or changed by the majority. It is this association that in effect is the highest governing body of the community. All owners are automatically members and have voices and votes in the deliberations and decisions of the association. (See Chapter 9.)

6. *Other advantages.* Many condominium owners may find satisfaction in the recent report from the Environmental Protection Agency, Department of Housing and Urban Development, and the Council on Environmental Quality. Issued in late 1974, the 278-page study concluded that high-density, planned residential areas such as condominium developments are much more economical and are more "environmentally advantageous" than single-family houses. Such communities are as much as 44 percent cheaper to build than the same number of individual houses, with most of the savings in the construction costs. Such communities generate up to 45 percent less air pollution, said the report. This is because high-density communities use less heat than single-family homes and require less automobile traffic.

Another often overlooked feature of high-density communities is reduction of water pollution. Storm water runoff from paved areas is a major source of such pollution, and there is far more of such paving in single-family housing than in condominium developments. The EPA study stated that developments could save up to 44 percent in energy consumption over low-density towns because of lower demands for house heating, air conditioning, and automobile use. Clustered communities also can save up to 35 percent on water use over single-family communities because, among other things, there are fewer lawns to water.

DISADVANTAGES

O.K., so condominiums sound as terrific as a new car guarantee. What's the catch?

The "catch" is not a catch. It is an entire collection of matters that we believe you should know about. Housing and communities are the most complicated structures created by man, and seldom, outside of Paradise, is perfection to be found. Here are some of the condominium disadvantages you should weigh.

1. *Community life style.* First off, condominium living is a distinct change of life style for nearly every new resident. Some critics call condominiums "communes with wall-to-wall carpeting." That overstates it, but the amount of privacy is definitely reduced. If you've never had close neighbors before, you're in for a new experience. They may be too close for comfort.

If the pitter-patter of little feet and the high-spirited shouts of youngsters distract you, you'd better check carefully the size of the juvenile population and/or restrictions against children before you buy your condominium. Furthermore, if the development is built around its major recreational facility—its pool, for instance—you're bound to hear every water sports noise except seal barking. If you are noise-sensitive, be sure to look carefully with this in mind as you shop for condominiums.

Example: "This whole place is a nightmare," complains a townhouse-owning widow in the ULI study. "The noise is constant. At 5:00 A.M. the sprinklers go on, then come the lawn mowers, then the noise of children with wagons, bikes, and balls—then the dogs and cats, with mothers screaming and yelling at children. We can't open our windows because of the noise, and there's no air conditioning here."

Another distinct change that you may find refreshing or disconcerting, depending on your psyche, is the change from the anonymity typical of high-rise apartment living. In the condominium development the community is closer-knit and residents generally know one another—or at least know a group of their fellow residents. This has its strengths and advantages, but for some people the move into "one big happy family" is unsettling.

If your individualistic soul says, "I must run barefooted and barebottomed through the garden every full moon," it *definitely* is not for you.

"Condominium living," comments David Froberg, president of a Chicago-based property management firm, "sometimes means bowing to the will of the majority as determined by the elected board of directors who run the project. This can be trouble if you own a dog and the majority bans pets or the board decides to raise your assessment fee to pay for new tennis courts and you don't play tennis."

2. *Homeowners' association (HOA).* Withdraw as you may, there is one aspect of condominium life you cannot safely avoid. That is the exercise of your responsibilities as a member of the HOA, the homeowners' association. There you will be, with your fellow condominium owners, thrown together by the chance circumstances and attractions of the project that drew all of you to purchase units.

As owners each of you has a stake in making the development work and an obligation to get together, organize, and elect leaders for the purpose of running it. This calls for cooperation and understanding and takes more time than you will have guessed. If you're accustomed to fighting the landlord every inch of the way for your rights as a tenant, you'll have to reverse your field, for the landlord of your condominium is, in large part, you. "We have met the enemy," as Pogo sagely observed, "and they is us."

There are aspects of the HOA that are unequal. For instance, you have a vote proportionate to your share of the common elements of the condominium. This fraction is defined in the contract, based on the value of your unit relative to all the others. So the owners of the largest and most expensive units may have shares four times the value of your own. That means their voting powers in the association will be four times yours. That can be a disadvantage, of course, when you favor one course of action and they cast their votes in opposition. The saving grace on this point is that owners of these units also have taxes and assessments four times as great as yours.[1]

To many condominium owners the periodic meetings of the HOA are all that they can cope with. (One condoleer quips, "Friendships that survive the first three general meetings of the HOA will last forever.") But from that group must come a board of directors of the project to oversee the condominium's continuing operation. In small developments this board may operate without hiring a professional manager. But as these amateur managers receive irate calls in the middle of the night about an overflowing toilet, a leaky roof, or a broken window, the joys and advantages of condominium life may begin to pall.

The board of directors is charged with running the entire development—letting contracts for landscaping, grounds keeping, operating recreational facilities, garbage disposal, common area upkeep, bookkeeping and financial management including insurance, reserves for contingencies (see

[1] The formulas used to determine voting power and undivided interest vary widely. This is typical of many, if not most.

Chapter 9, section on boards and committees), etc. Board members have to decide hot questions such as who pays for installing underground garbage cans and rock salt for sidewalks, for instance. If the legal documents for the condominium are fuzzy on such matters, roaring community arguments may result. Inflamed tempers endanger future cooperation. All of these are considerations that persuade many HOAs to hire professional managers.

Example: "As far as I know, the home association here has a list of a hundred and fifty items for the builder to make good on," charges the owner of a $20,000 townhouse in the ULI study. "For six months nothing has been done because of the lousy board of directors we have."

Patience, as you can see, is a virtue sometimes required. The art of compromise may be a skill you will have to develop. Also acceptance: Much as you may wish to change the exterior of your unit from white clapboard to purple tile with sequins, the basic condominium declaration and by-laws very likely stipulate what, if any, changes may be made. And sequins, we'll bet, aren't included. You'll have to accept what cannot be changed through amendment of the by-laws.

Example: "The salesmen did not tell us about the association rules before we bought," complains one owner in the ULI study. "The outside of our home is blah and we bought with the idea we could fix it up. After we bought we found we could not. We have a twelve-hundred-dollar TV set but can't use the hundred-and-thirty-dollar aerial that we need to get good reception. The by-laws should have been mentioned before we bought."

3. *Maintenance.* This factor is so important that it often becomes a major tension area. Owners have differing ideas about what maintenance is included and who maintains what.

The quality of maintenance also comes in for severe criticism. "Blindfolded they cut the grass," growls one perfectionist. "I sold all my tools when I sold my house," laments another owner who believed the ads for "carefree living." "But now I just bought them back—the maintenance here is for the birds!"

Owner complaints on this subject relate directly, of course, to association dues: what part of the budget is devoted to maintenance and the extent and quality of the maintenance performed. They also relate to the original budget for the condominium project with its spellout of the association dues, maintenance, insurance, and reserve fees quoted by the salesmen when the units were first marketed.

Consider this comment from one unit owner in the ULI survey: "Association fees cost me two hundred fifty-seven dollars annually. This is unnecessary and is an added living expense. I would prefer being responsible for exterior maintenance on my home. The 'private' pool is a duplicate expense, since it is no longer private because of the large membership and since the county has a public pool nearby which my taxes help maintain."

This man's misconceptions about what a condominium is and what his fees are for are so vast it is doubtful he'll ever be satisfied as a condominium owner. Obviously the developer never sufficiently explained his responsibilities as a condominium owner or what his fees were to pay for. (See Chapter 9.)

Generally, maintenance fees cover such services as trash, leaf, and snow removal, upkeep of common areas and equipment, grounds, walks, streets, parking areas, roofs, hallways, heating plant, recreation facilities. Almost invariably the original estimates of monthly charges are low. Not until the condominium has been in operation after all the units are sold, the tax assessment has been set, and the developer has severed his connection with the project is it usually possible to get a completely accurate fix on the continuing charges.

New owners move into a development and at a certain point, when a stated number or percentage of the units is sold, the deed to all common grounds and buildings is turned over by the developer to the owners' association. As control passes, so does responsibility for maintaining the grounds and buildings, of managing the development. Up until this point the developer may have picked up all or part of these expenses. Suddenly the owners are on their own and the dimly perceived responsibilities and full costs of unsubsidized maintenance are thrust upon them. More often than not it's a rude jolt.

RED FLAG: Builders tend to state condominium maintenance costs on the low side. Their salesmen may "forget" expense elements in giving prospects estimates of costs.

Even buyers who are sophisticated and knowledgeable about the law sometimes are tripped up. Robert E. De Mascio, judge of the United States District Court in Detroit, bought a condominium in a new high-rise building in February 1973. A year later he filed suit to break his contract to purchase the $52,000 unit. Reason? At the time he bought, he was quoted $155 a month as the figure to cover parking, maintenance, and building personnel costs. Before the first year was over the charges soared to $234 and Judge De Mascio wanted out. He charged that the developer had made "false inducement" in grossly understating the real maintenance and other monthly costs. (At this writing the case has not been decided.)

Unfortunately, in almost nine out of ten cases buyers have no recourse except costly, time-consuming lawsuits such as this if they believe they have been taken. State laws are notably loose on this matter. New York State is an exception; there the state's attorney general forced one builder to return $555,000 to purchasers of eighteen condominium units. The developer had deliberately deceived by understating real estate taxes on the units.

4. *Leasing.* A condominium disadvantage of major, even scandalous, proportions is leasing. (See Chapter 9.) In Florida leasing of land, parking space, and recreational facilities is common. In FHA-approved condominiums it is outlawed.

RED FLAG: Florida's high-rise condominium contracts usually include a clause that gives the builder a ninety-nine-year lease on such elements as the swimming pool, for instance. Some contracts include automatic cost-of-living increases that jack up owner costs. The monthly payments may start out low. But the developer can change them—and does. Furthermore, these leases are written into your master deed as mechanics' liens, which take precedence over even your mortgage payments. This means simply that if you refuse to pay, the leaseholder can go to court and force you to pay and/or eventually evict you or cause your unit to be sold to satisfy his claims.

Example: A classic case is that of the builder who installed a pool and recreational facilities at a cost of $1 million. He then charged those who bought units in the huge development $3.5 million *per year* for the use of these facilities. All perfectly legal, in Florida.

Florida developers defend leasing. They say it makes it possible for the builder to sell condominium units at lower prices than if he sold the leased land or facilities along with the units. Sure: He's selling the units cheap, but getting a built-in set of captive clients for his leased property on which he alone sets the prices and reaps the profits. It's the old "company store" concept gone modern.

5. *Rentals.* If a sizable portion of the units in the develop-

ment is rented out by the developer (perhaps because he cannot sell them), you may find yourself in an overgrown motel rather than a condominium community. The danger is that the tenants, feeling little responsibility to treat their quarters as homes, do not care for them in the same fashion as owners. As the quality of the units deteriorates, so does their value. Owners, seeing the trend, place their units on the market and the prices for the units decline. A wholesale rush to unload may be triggered.

Example: "We have a tremendous turnover here," reports the owner of a $25,000 townhouse in the ULI study. "Realtors buy and rent to undesirable families who don't care; the yard is not kept up. The typical renter has no consideration for others—they race their cars, play loud music in the evenings, allow their dogs to run outside and bark late. Realtors who buy should not be allowed to rent to just anyone. We are moving as soon as we can, since there are few actual homeowners left and the neighborhood is going to pot."

In this chapter we've looked at some of the more important condominium advantages and disadvantages. We've included them to help you weigh condominium life before deciding whether it is or is not for you. It's a new life style and we believe it has definite advantages for Americans in the coming decades. But though the positives far outnumber the negatives in our view, we believe you should be aware of the drawbacks. You'll find more specifics on the hazards of buying in the next chapter.

PRO AND CONDO

A comparison between a condominium and a private house of similar size, rooms, features, and construction quality on its own plot of land generally looks something like this:

Condominium Advantages	Private House Advantages
Lower cost.	
Easier financing through developer.	
Possibility of rental with option to buy.	
Security of neighbors nearby, guards, TV monitor, other security devices, patrols.	Privacy and possible isolation.
Continuous maintenance, freedom from chores.	Freedom to treat exterior as you please.
Quick access to repairs.	
Share in community amenities, such as tennis courts, swimming pools.	Freedom from assessment for unwanted facilities.
	No complications with builder or agent; no problem with incomplete execution of promises; no conflict with other owners in association.
Public transportation in or near larger condominiums.	
If you rent your unit, management often helps in making arrangements.	
	Title passes at closing. Condominium title may wait months after occupancy.

5

En Garde!

The fellow that owns his own home is always just coming out of a hardware store.

—Frank Hubbard

The voice at the other end of the line is warm and friendly. Just a bit too friendly for a perfect stranger. "Hello," it coos. "This is Harry Nardle calling from Mumblesport, just up the coast from Disneyworld. Have you been to Disneyworld?"

You sift your memory, trying to recognize the voice. Is it the same man who tried to sell you an Edsel? Or five hundred shares of Penn Central stock?

"Well, you must know that Oogaloosa County is the fastest growing county in the U.S. And I'm calling you about the greatest investment-retirement-leisure-living opportunity in fifty years"—pause—"Orange Heaven—one hundred thousand pond- and palm-covered sun-kissed acres of fabulous condominiums. . . . You do like oranges, don't you?"

You grunt affirmatively.

"Well, we have a free orange for you if you'll just come on down and see our beautiful condos, our championship golf course, our six-hundred-thousand-dollar yacht club, Olympic pool, night-and-day tennis, surf-casting, boating, jai-alai, and dog-racing paradise. After seeing them, you'll be begging to invest from thirty-seven thousand dollars up in one of our dynamic Vista-View condos. . . ."

Sound familiar?

If you haven't had telephone calls from Harry Nardle, you must have received the handsome mailing pieces—the glossy, full-color illustrations on paper so slick you need suction cups to hold it. If by some odd oversight you've never received either these enticing phone calls *or* mailings, you could scarcely overlook the billboards, magazine and newspaper ads, and, in some areas, the TV commercials. The pitches have certain common themes:

"Not just a place to live, but a place to come alive . . ."

"Truly not for everyone, but for those who demand the ultimate . . ."

"Miracle in nearby Nassau County. Why rent when you can own a beautiful three-bedroom townhouse condominium residence for only two hundred fifty-two a month?"

"We have it all: Spectacular condominium homes. A country-club environment. Idyllic location. And mortgages."

"Practically jutting into the sea [in reality three blocks away] . . . twenty-one stories of superb views . . . privacy . . . your own resort and recreation club . . . unprecedented seclusion too." (In one of those twenty-one stories?)

One observation comes immediately to anyone exposed to a few condominium ads: Hyperbole is alive and thriving in this industry. It is to be expected. Housing ads are like perfume ads: the words are often more powerful than the reality. So if the sales literature calls it a patio, a loggia, a verandah, or a deck, even though it's a 4′ × 8′ balcony, recognize that it isn't a country estate at Marienbad you're buying. Enjoy it, but don't be carried away by the romance of the words.

After all, the products being peddled by developers are the most expensive items on the market in the United States: homes. Automobiles sell at only a pale fraction of the price. You're no doubt aware of the remarkable claims made for every widely advertised product from alcohol to zippers. Chances are that you haven't believed everything they've claimed since you gave up Santa Claus. The Federal Trade Commission, a government regulatory agency, rides herd on the ads of auto makers, drug and pharmaceutical producers, food and clothing marketers. The FTC often jumps on the most outrageous claims and forces advertisers to prove the claims—to put up or shut up. And still the general level of product advertising requires a skeptical attitude.

In condominium advertising, where the dollar value is so much greater, and the unbridled claims range from extraordinary through spectacular to the celestial, the FTC has yet to shoulder its burden. It has not taken action to keep condo merchants honest. Only in mid-1974 did the agency announce a nationwide study of condominium marketing practices. Its major excuse for not acting to protect consumers has been that most condominium units are sold within a state, not across state lines, and therefore are not subject to federal regulation.

Nevertheless, the FTC study should result in action by the agency or recommendations for legislation or both. Meanwhile, congressmen have been prodded by angry constituents in several parts of the nation and a number of bills have been introduced to make full disclosure mandatory, with serious penalties for misrepresentation. It is to be hoped that soon there will be federal laws to help protect condominium buyers.

"More people are swindled in this county than anywhere else in the United States, but we have never yet indicted a developer." These strong words were spoken by Philip Montante, assistant state's attorney in charge of consumer fraud in Broward County in southern Florida. His views are shared by many experts familiar with the condominium craze that has overwhelmed much of Florida. The charges leveled against some Florida developers (not all of them, of course) go far beyond misleading advertising to shoddy construction, blood-sucking leases on recreation facilities, hidden costs sprung on the purchaser *after* he's bought, and exaggerated promises about investment returns.

Even if or when the federal government steps in with

protective measures, you'll still need to keep your wits about you when shopping for a condominium. We have suggestions that may help keep you *en garde* to avoid possible grief.

1. *Background information.* The key to making a sound purchase is reliable information. You need all of it you can get. The seller will give you plenty of advertising literature, and you will see his ads in newspapers. You need more impartial information than that from other sources. Such as?

A. The FHA is the best. Ask the seller if any of his units are FHA-insured. If so, this is a big plus. FHA is short for the Federal Housing Administration of the U.S. Department of Housing and Urban Development. FHA has programs offering mortgage insurance to condominium developers and/or owners whose units qualify. The regulations are stringent, intended to protect the buyer and the government. For example, the FHA will not approve projects where recreation or other facilities are leased.

Essentially, you can be sure that if the condominium has FHA backing it satisfies rigid federal requirements. Therefore, you as a buyer know that the financing is sound and at bargain rates, the construction is good, and the purchase agreement, master deed, by-laws, management agreement, and regulatory agreement are all legal, fair, and equitable, because they have been examined, reviewed, and approved by FHA experts.

Since this is so, the condominium bargain hunter will look first for an FHA-insured project or unit. Unfortunately there aren't enough of them available. Fewer than 5 percent of all new construction mortgages in 1974 were FHA-insured. The reasons are several, but the main ones are (*a*) because of the red tape involved, many builders don't wish to construct FHA-insured projects; (*b*) FHA has ceilings on the mortgages for units it helps finance, and in these inflationary times many builders consider the FHA limits too low to be practical; and (*c*) FHA places upper limits on the interest rate that may be charged on mortgages it insures. These limits are almost always below the going rate in the money market, so banks and savings and loan associations often are unwilling to undertake FHA-insured loans, especially in tight-money times.

The FHA has offices in every state in the union. Ask your local banker for the address of the closest one. The FHA's head office: Federal Housing Administration, Department of Housing and Urban Development, 451 7th Street, S.W., Washington, D.C.

B. The Office of Interstate Land Sales Registration of the U.S. Department of Housing and Urban Development (HUD) can require full disclosure in sales of land across state lines. But developers can easily dodge this by contracting to build a structure on the land within two years of the date you sign the sales contract.

If the developer has followed the registration procedure, ask him for the HUD Property Report. This document is required for sellers of land in interstate commerce. It is an abbreviated treatment of the official legal statement filed with the Office of Interstate Land Sales Registration. In the Property Report the seller must disclose who owns the development company and details about the property, including information about parts under water or impossible to build upon without considerable improvement—and the kind of improvements necessary. HUD regulations require that every interstate buyer be offered such a Property Report before purchase. *The sale can be voided if the buyer has not been given the Property Report.*

OILSR's address: Office of Interstate Land Sales Registration, Department of Housing and Urban Development, 451 7th Street, S.W., Washington, D.C.

C. The Securities and Exchange Commission (SEC) seems a peculiar agency to be involved in condominium sales regulations. It is concerned with condominiums that are promoted as investments, intended to provide a return.

Typically, these are resort or vacation condominium units

in which the developer promises/suggests/arranges to rent out your unit when you are not using it and promises/suggests that you will make a profit—or receive income. If he sells you the unit first and *then* suggests that you might profit from renting it out, and also that it may increase in value over the years, the SEC probably can't do a thing. Over the years, only sixty-nine such resort condominiums had registered by mid-1974.

It is unfortunate that SEC regulations on disclosure do not apply across the board to all condominium sales. They are exacting and require full disclosure of the type a corporation must give when it floats an issue of stock. This means detailed data about the organization, its officers and principals, the items being marketed (in this case the units) with full descriptions, physical and financial, the entire cost structure of building, marketing, and profits, as well as the projected rental scheme with full spellout of the rents to be charged, the management fees, the competition to be expected, and much, much more. All this information is included in the prospectus required by the SEC. Until this legal document is received and registered with the SEC, the units cannot be sold in interstate trade.

So ask the developer for a copy of the SEC prospectus for the project. But don't be surprised if he tells you there is none, since so few condominiums are covered. If you doubt him, write the SEC, 500 North Capitol, Street, Washington, D.C., and ask if the development is registered.

D. The Federal Trade Commission (FTC) could move against developers who are deceiving customers. It could also set down a broad rule that would apply across the board in condominium marketing. However, it is limited to interstate sales. And whatever it does probably won't help you with your specific problem today. You may want to remember it's there, in case you need to complain about the practices of some developer. Write: Federal Trade Commission, Pennsylvania Avenue at 6th Street, N.W., Washington, D.C.

O.K., you've looked and there are no FHA condominiums available in your area, no OILSR, no SEC, no FTC help. What next? Time to ask for the prospectus required by the state.

E. The prospectus is a legal document, a public offering statement filed with the state real estate authorities. In it the builder/developer is required to disclose who is selling, what he is selling, and the circumstances or features affecting the project. It is in this document that you'll find such essentials as the basic deed, projected taxes, expenses, and assessments for one year, terms of financing offered to buyers, warranties (if any), zoning and other restrictions, any agreements affecting the property and your right to the common elements of it, and much more. In some states no contract to purchase a condominium is valid unless you sign a statement that you've received this prospectus. (Nobody can force you to read it, but the state wants to make sure you have these facts before you buy.)

As we noted earlier, some states have far stronger real estate laws than others. In such states as New York, Virginia, Michigan, California, and Hawaii the public offering statements are tremendously helpful to the condominium hunter because they include more vital information than do permissive states.

F. Zoning authorities and the town engineer or building inspector are good places to check on the local level—to make sure local ordinances and building code regulations have been met. A gorgeous brochure for a waterfront condominium on Long Island Sound so excited a friend of ours that he called the town engineer of the locality where this handsome, expensive complex was situated. It was being advertised lavishly in local newspapers and regional magazines as the answer to a sybarite's prayer.

"You must be the patient type," said the engineer. "Let's see ... bulkheads are needed and that whole shore comes under the new federal sound preservation program. The Corps of Engineers has to be satisfied too. And then the state wants to make sure the coastline is not endangered. Of course our town has construction regulations that have to be met. . . . You're not anxious to move in soon, are you?"

His estimate was that when federal, state, and local authorities and the army had each approved and the construction was actually completed, everyone concerned would be four or five years older. Obviously information from the building inspector or engineer can be extremely helpful.

A call to the local zoning board secretary or town clerk can help you find out whether there are any pending or postponed problems with the development. Also you may wish to visit Town Hall to read the zoning board minutes concerning the public hearings about the project: if there were strong fundamental reasons for delaying the development, such as inadequate plans for sewage disposal or surface water control. Zoning board minutes will tell how the problems were met —or circumvented. An alternative to this is a visit to the local library or newspaper office. There you can consult the issues of the local paper that report on the original project proposal and its pros and cons, objections and opposition from the neighbors, and so on.

G. The local tax assessor's office is another helpful port of call. The assessor can tell you if the developer has built other housing in the community. In many towns the assessor not only establishes a market price for a housing unit, he also determines and grades the quality of construction, the basic materials used, and workmanship. By consulting his records he may be able to inform you of the rating of your builder's previous projects, if not the current one.

You *should* be concerned about the builder, especially if you are shopping for a condominium that is in the planning stage or still under construction. Unless you are familiar with building and architecture, you are at a distinct disadvantage in figuring out from plans or half-built structures whether the final result will be as promised in the pretty brochures, ads, and salesmen's words. The builder/developer supplies more than enough promises. Your question has to be: Does he deliver?

H. The state real estate commission will help you find out if the builder has met all state requirements. Has he completed any other condominiums, apartments, or multiunit developments? You'll want to know what the results were. The real estate commission can tell you where and when. Ask if there is any record of criminal or noncriminal processes or adverse orders issued to the builder concerning any of his projects and details of such proceedings. The commission will have such information. If there have been none, he may be clean. Or it may be that other projects were built under another corporate name. You'll have to ask about each such corporation. This is where your bank can help.

I. Your local banker can get information about the developer's company and its principal officers from his correspondent bank in the company's headquarters town. We strongly recommend that you invest in a Dun and Bradstreet report on the builder/developer.

Your bank will order the report, charge you for it (under $10), and tell you what it reveals. Among other things, it will tell the corporate names used, the business history, the financial strength, and the credit standing of the company and its key officers. You may find that they're in hock up to their elbows and haven't enough money to shovel the streets of their project, much less finish the construction.

J. The people probe is another big help. People who live in projects built by the same developer can provide firsthand information about his delivery on his promises. Do you like to snoop? Thrive on gossip? Then you'll enjoy the role of unofficial investigator. We have found it extremely useful to interview residents. They tell it "like it is." More often than not you'll find they tend to stress the negatives, the shortcomings, irritations, unkept promises, lapses in design or workmanship. All of this may be good to know sooner rather than when it's too late.

2. *On-site inspection: the walkabout.* Nothing can substitute for a visit to the site. There you'll actually be able to determine the lay of the land and your reaction to it. Until then, all the photos and words can't convey what your senses can tell you in minutes. You'll probably respond positively. But you may be turned off by the whole arrangement.

Then there are the specifics of the complex itself. Outside the four walls of your unit, what would life be like in this development? The on-site walkabout is useful to size up the setup. It will familiarize you with the terrain, the setting, the features, convenience or lack thereof, and other key matters. With project map in hand, go over the landscape. In the process, check out the following:

A. Location of project in the community: How far to existing public transportation? If none exists, where will projected public transportation be? (Don't forget to ask when—and who says?) How far to the school bus stop? To the nearest services and provisions you'll need as bare minimums—pharmacy, market, hardware store, laundry and dry cleaning, luncheonette.

B. Location of unit within the project: Imaginative placement of the units in the landscape can make a development appealing—or depressing—to live in. Research studies indicate that housing units clustered around courtyards promote a sense of community. Residents of such developments are significantly more active in community affairs and (it is said) rarely complain.

In contrast, residents of ribbon-like row houses have poor attendance records at homeowners' association meetings, are notorious grumblers, and generally go to meetings mainly to air gripes rather than to participate in positive planning. Developers have found that there are more callbacks and the resale rate is faster in row houses. So in your walkabout, study the layout of the units. If it is a cluster development, are the clusters arranged attractively? Are the arrangements practical? Is the traffic pattern logical and efficient?

If it is a row development, are the rows arranged monotonously one after the other? Is there enough space around each unit? What are the views from inside? If the complex is large, is it broken up into small, cozy neighborhoods, or is it one long, boring, impersonal mass? How secluded and wooded is the complex? Are there green belts to provide diversity and eye interest?

Another purpose of your walkabout is to determine how your unit will fit into the scheme of things. Friends of ours bought an expensive luxury condominium in the woods, complete with floor-to-ceiling glass windows on one living-room wall, so they could enjoy the sight of the trees and birds and squirrels. They wound up with a panoramic view of the project's incinerator! You might find yourself with an equally charming outlook on the garbage collection site. Or the laundry facility. Or a maintenance shed. Or a neighbor's kitchen. Or a soon-to-be-built high-rise apartment that cuts off your view entirely.

If you can't tell from the site drawings, ask the sales people for specific information. If there's any doubt in your mind, your best bet is to go over the plans with an architect and have him check out such matters.

C. Safety elements and health hazards: We have called this a walkabout with good reason. We're serious when we suggest you do it on foot, rather than from the comfort of an automobile or an armchair. In the process of walking you'll learn a good deal about the site, the convenience to various facilities, and the quality of the planning that went into the development. It is good to measure these distances in human, experiential terms rather than via vehicle or diagram. At some time you'll need to know some of these things, if not all. How far from your unit is the nearest fire hydrant? This can affect your insurance rate. Are there areas designated for casual walking, for play, for rest and relaxing? As you wander the grounds, does the faint music of a thousand mosquitoes rising from the damp grass tell you that you're going to be needled mercilessly all summer long? If you have young children, that picturesque but unguarded pond could be a disaster area.

A check list of safety factors is essential. Are there guard rails on stairs? Are there areas on the grounds where toddly young legs or shaky old ones might falter? Are tot lots close enough to the buildings for mothers to watch the children? These are just starters on the list of questions you'll want to ask.

D. Parking facilities: This is a serious matter in viewing and reviewing condominiums. Inadequate parking is an almost universal complaint among condominium owners. In California, where condominium units generally have carports or garages, the complaints are as bitter as in the East, where open-air parking is more common. Developments given high grades in all other areas are often criticized for inadequate or poorly planned parking facilities. You can check this out easily—by looking for yourself, talking with owners, and getting the specific facts from the developer.

Parking space should be provided at the rate of two spaces per family *minimum,* with additional guest parking areas. There should be a separate area on the grounds for campers, trailers, or other recreation vehicles. It may be off-site. The reasons are several. The two most important are: (1) the size of such vehicles—they take up valuable parking space—and (2) they are unsightly to many people, indicating an objectionable, unsettled camp-out ambience.

E. Density: "The lower the density, the higher the owner satisfaction" is the condominium axiom used by planners. How many units is the developer planning in all? On how much land? If the project looks complete, but the developer owns countless acres of greenery next door to the project, find out what else might be lurking on his drawing board. The swimming pool may comfortably accommodate the hundred units in the current project, but if he adds a second project— with pool rights—to the first, then overcrowding could be a real problem. It's happened.

Density and the sense of being crowded are to a high degree psychological. Densities as high as seventeen units per acre are acceptable to buyers of townhouses if there are open spaces, views, and green areas—even if they are not a part of the project. So seafront developments can, in general, stand greater density. Projects well placed in and around golf courses also may have more units and still satisfy the owners. However, residents are not impressed with open space several blocks away; they need the feeling of space when looking out from their own units.

Another factor is the total number of units in the development. In general, the larger the development, the greater the sense of crowding—even if the density is not more than six or seven units per acre. Before you buy, know the ultimate size of the project. If the project is surrounded by woods and greenery, tucked into a rolling hillside, find out if this is only temporary, an illusion. It can be. The sound of bulldozers may be heard in the land—but perhaps not until after you've signed your contract. By then it's a little late to discover that three other projects are going up all around you, making a complete condominium city. This may suit you to a T (for townhouse). But then again, it may not. Better to know ahead of time what the projections are for the next few months, if not the next twenty years. If you're settling in Serenity Woods, better be sure the woodland beyond your project is going to stay that way. How do you find out? That's one more question to ask the oracle—the salesman who's doing his best to lure you to his dotted line.

3. *What to ask the oracle—questions for the salesman.* We can't underscore enough the importance of gathering all the information you can. We've stressed that you should get the property report or prospectus for the project and read it through and through until you understand it thoroughly. No doubt there will still be unanswered questions. Your source of immediate answers, the oracle on the spot, is the salesman. Put your questions to him. But do these three things: (1) Carry

a small notebook; (2) make note of the salesman's name; and (3) jot down his answers. You'll find that these precautions will make him more accurate. And your notes may be useful to you at some later time in case of misunderstanding or dispute.

Here are some key questions for him.

A. If you buy before the project is completed, does your payment go into an escrow account? If the salesman says yes, ask him to show you where the contract says so. What is an escrow account? It's a bank account that the builder/developer cannot touch until he has fulfilled contract requirements. Why is escrow important? Because if the builder/developer goes broke or stops before completing the project, your money is still safe in that escrow account. You'll get it back. If it isn't protected this way, you may lose it all.

B. Ask the salesman for the budget for the project and the breakdown of costs per unit. *Beware low-balling.* To make the deal attractive, salesmen have a tendency to underestimate or understate costs, taxes, and prices. Insist on seeing the budget in writing. (See Chapter 6.) You know the budget must include your payment (on a monthly basis) of mortgage principal, interest, taxes, and insurance. It also must include continuing payments for management fees and costs, maintenance of common elements and recreational features, and reserve fund for replacement of roofs, boilers, asphalt, and so on, plus contingencies.

Analyze this budget and determine whether it is realistic in today's market. Check with someone skilled in the field, if possible, such as a real estate professional, apartment manager, architect, accountant, or banker.

RED FLAG: There may be a number of jokers in the budget. For instance, are the streets in the project to be maintained by you and your fellow owners? Or are they to be maintained by the city? Ask the salesman that one; the answer could be expensive to you if the project has to maintain them.

RED FLAG: How about recreational maintenance costs? Take swimming pools: are town regulations covered in the costs? For instance, if the town demands attendance by a lifeguard at each public pool, are salaries for the guards included in the pool budget?

C. What provisions have been made for insurance? Usually the condominium declaration provides for a master hazard policy. This insures against casualty and fire losses and certain other disasters. But there are more hazards than these to be covered. The pool, tennis courts, central air conditioning, elevator—all of these are possible sources of damage to property and people and should be covered. Furthermore, personal property and liability protection are needed by each unit owner on a separate, individual policy.

The question is: How much will your share of the overall condominium policy be, and how much will your individual policy cost?

RED FLAG: Until 1974 no insurance policy specifically tailored to condominium needs existed. Policies simply cut and pasted assemblages from other policies covering apartments, houses, and so on. They left a lot of bases uncovered. Be sure to ask whether the master policy is specifically written for condominiums.

Incidentally, some insurance companies offer a discount on the individual owner policies if the condominium association sponsors the fire and theft package. Inquire about this also.

D. Ask about the reserve fund. The monthly assessments for this fund are often woefully inadequate, sometimes non-existent. The developer/seller generally would rather not talk about this because it opens up too many problem areas for him. For instance, the higher the reserve fund assessment, the more your monthly payments will be and the less attractive the condominium may appear. The higher the reserve fund, the more questions are raised in the minds of potential buyers: Why so much for roof replacement? Is it made cheaply? Is it faulty? The XYZ project didn't have any roof replacement fund set aside (or had a lower amount set aside). Ditto for the heating plant and other depreciable parts of the project.

What *should* the reserve fund amount be? Unfortunately, there is no solid way to answer that. No rule-of-thumb percentage of total project or unit cost fits all condominiums. The limitless variety of climatic conditions, building materials, architectural designs, and user wear and tear involved make such a rule impossible. The galloping inflation of recent years has not made it easier, either. But you must begin somewhere, and replacement costs and expected life tables for elements such as roofs, boilers, motors, and heating plants should have been used by the developer as bases for projecting reserve requirements. Ask for this projection and check it out with a specialist—banker, apartment manager, or architect.

E. How about leased feature payments? Do you have to pay for the use of parking space? For recreational facilities? Any other extras? If so, does the sales contract include a clause stating clearly what is leased, what your share of the payments will be, and what control (if any) there is over escalation of these fees? The lease property gimmick can be the most expensive rip-off condominium buyers suffer. The FHA and New York State laws prohibit such leasing, but it is common in Florida and other states. It is called a leasehold clause. Be aware of it, protest it, and—the ultimate weapon—don't buy! Or buy in a state with tougher laws.

F. Project stability: Is there any plan to enlarge the project at a later date? Whatever the salesman's answer to this, ask him to point out the place in the prospectus or sales contract that says so one way or the other. This could be a fast curve. Why?

Example: After you've settled into your new home in the

condominium project, the developer erects a commercial building next door. It has an around-the-clock pizza stand, an all-night discotheque, a bowling alley, and a shooting gallery (the old-fashioned kind with rifles). You may not like it, but his right to do this is spelled out in the fine print of the prospectus and/or sales contract. You're stuck.

Example: Some time after completion of the residences the developer begins additional construction. What's he up to? He's building a luxury marina and yacht club (or golf course or you-name-it). Dandy, but you never touch the stuff. Who will share the costs and upkeep of this expensive new facility? Why, you and your fellow condominium owners, that's who—unless the prospectus or sales contract makes it clear that there are no "add-ons" of this or any other sort permitted.

G. Rentals—another potential disaster area. If this is not a resort condominium, can the units be rented to transients? FHA regulations prohibit such rental of family unit condominiums, for good reason. The definition of transient rental is a period of less than thirty days. (This does not rule out leasing your unit for normal residential purposes by the year.)

What can happen if this type of rental is allowed is best described as accelerated decay. The developer may find himself with a sizable number of units unsold and decide to rent them out on any basis he can, simply to bring in needed cash. Transients, with no commitment to maintain the premises, cause more wear and tear than residents do, and sometimes are nuisances to boot. The character of the condominium can be affected by such revolving-door types. Property values deteriorate, along with the common elements, and one after another owners flee the foundering ship. (Under FHA regulations one person may own no more than four units in a project.)

H. Documents: be sure to review the purchase agreement

with the salesman. It should conform to state laws covering sales contracts. It should either include or refer to the master deed or declaration, the by-laws, a budget, schedule of estimated monthly costs, and other documents that are part of the sales contract. *But it is no substitute for these documents,* which must disclose all the facts about the condominium and must be furnished to you before the sale is completed. (See Chapter 6.) The purchase agreement will state under what conditions your down payment may be returned to you, and when it may be claimed by the seller. Be sure to ask about these vital conditions before you sign and turn over your check.

RED FLAG: Beware of signing any kind of purchase agreement or binder that ratifies documents you have not read thoroughly and understood. Sometimes these agreements try to wing a fast ball past you, slipping in clauses such as "purchaser is deemed liable for his share of costs for extras and changes, whether structural or superficial." That kind of language means you'll be hit for costs incurred by the builder in changes he may want to make, whether you and the other condominium owners want them or not. If there is any language in the purchase agreement that you don't understand clearly, take it to your lawyer for review *before you sign it.*

I. What is your share of responsibility (undivided interest percentage) established for the unit you're considering? Is there any language in the agreement or other documents that makes it possible to change unit ratios in the future? These are extremely important questions that you will skip at your peril. Here's why.

The share of responsibility (undivided interest) formula determines:

1. What portion/percentage of the common area(s) you own.

2. The amount you'll be assessed for maintenance and operation of the condominium.

3. Your share of the real estate taxes.

4. How many votes you have in the homeowners' association.

5. The amount of the mortgage a bank or loan association will grant on your unit and your share of the common elements.

The state's condominium law may spell out what formula must be used for establishing your share of the undivided interest. There are three basic methods: by size, by value or market price, and by equal slices.

If by *size*, your unit's living area as a fraction of the total of all units' living areas gives you your percentage of total votes, assessments, taxes, etc. (i.e., yours = 5,000 square feet; total project = 500,000 square feet; thus your share = 1/100 or 1 percent).

If by *value or market price*, your unit's value or price as a fraction of the total of all units' values or prices determines your percentage of the total (i.e., yours = $30,000; total = $3,000,000; thus your share = 1/100 or 1 percent).

If by *equal shares*, your votes, assessments, taxes, etc., are the same as those of every other unit (i.e., in a project of 100 units, yours would be 1/100 or 1 percent).

RED FLAG: There is a danger in any language in the contract that makes it possible to change this share of responsibility. The danger is that you may find yourself with a larger percentage than you expected when you bought. It's true that this would give you a larger vote in the HOA. But it also would increase your taxes and assessments. That means money, honey.

Ask the salesman specifically what the limits of your property as a unit owner are. Does the property extend beyond the coat of paint on the walls and ceiling and the covering on the floor? In other words, if the plumbing or wiring goes bad beyond the walls, floor, or ceiling of your unit, who is responsible for repair costs—you or the HOA? And where do your maintenance responsibilities end? Friends of ours bought a condominium in which they are responsible for keeping the windows clean inside and out, even though one of these is a sealed picture window six by eight feet—nine feet above the ground! Needless to say, it isn't washed often.

We suggest that you ask the salesman window-and-door questions: Who washes the exteriors? Who paints and repairs them? Who puts on screens and keeps them in good repair?

J. How good are you at reading plans and visualizing architectural drawings? You'll need such skills in checking out the floor plans and site plans of your condominium if it is still under construction or at the preconstruction stage. Your best bet is to have an architect actually go over the floor plan with you and show you on the site what the drawings indicate. You'll be glad you did, even if there's a model room on display and an architectural model shows the layout of the finished project. Why?

Example: Did you ever see a bed only five feet long? No, we don't mean in a midget's house. The last time we saw one was in the bedroom of a model unit for a 250-unit development. The model unit was lovely, decorated by a professional, furnished lavishly by one of New York's leading furniture stores. The total effect was beautiful, elegant enough to be a screen set. But a five-foot bed? That's right. It had been specially cut down by the developer to make the bedroom look larger. And further measuring revealed that the sofa, coffee table, and sideboard were undersized, the kitchen counter was twenty inches deep instead of the standard twenty-four, and the dining-room-table legs had been shortened to twenty-seven inches instead of the usual thirty to make the low ceiling appear higher. All in all, it was, as they say, a great place to visit, but you wouldn't want to live there.

The point is, sometimes you can't even trust your eyes. Take along a pocket rule when you visit the model unit. If room dimensions are given in the sales literature, check them. You may discover that the measurements are from the edge of the eaves instead of the inside wall of the unit. Some sharp operators give the dimensions of the entire length of the unit, leaving it up to you to discover that the kitchen is really only wide enough to mince through sideways because it's four feet across. Another favorite ploy is to include the closet in the room measurement. You may find that what appears to be a wall in the floor plan turns out to be a vertical "planting area" or folding screen in the completed unit.

We urge you to measure the model unit and record its dimensions room by room, including ceiling height. Record these measurements on the floor plan. They should be the same. If they're not, be sure the seller specifies what you're buying—the floor-plan specifications or the model specs. Just so you both agree on what's being bought and sold.

Remember also that display models may be larger than life. For example, many times they are built on oversize lots with more space around them than you will receive in your unit. Also, they may be equipped with elements not included in the finished units, such as special lighting fixtures. What's even worse, sometimes model units are displayed with features *specifically prohibited* by the declaration and by-laws —such as covered patios and outside trellises. Take your notebook in hand and ask the salesman about such exterior elements, if they are important to you. If he says they are included or can be, ask him to show you the paragraph in the by-laws that say so. Ask and you shall receive—sometimes.

4. *Final inspection.* After you've gone through the intricate and exhausting process of comparison shopping and have finally contracted to buy a new condominium, the time will come when the developer will call you to inspect and O.K. it. At this critical moment you can blow much of the

time, effort, and money you've invested in the deal—unless you are careful.

Ideally, you should examine the entire place with someone skilled in house construction—a contractor/builder/architect/engineer. You need someone who knows what to look for in checking out a new housing unit. In most towns a certificate of occupancy is required before you may live in a new housing unit. Town regulations vary. In some, you can't move in until the building inspector approves the structure. In others you may move in but the building inspector's O.K. is required within a certain specified time period.

RED FLAG: Cosmetic alterations. Beware of temporary changes made by the builder right before the inspector's brief visit.

A friend of ours had already moved into his new home when the builder's men removed the window air conditioner and put it in the garage—just minutes before the building inspector arrived. The 12-inch overhang of the air conditioner would have violated the city's regulations about minimum clearance from the property line. The air conditioner was reinstalled the next day, and our friend has been "living in sin"—in violation of the city building code—ever since.

When the developer calls, ask him if the building inspector has issued a certificate of occupancy. If he has, fine. If he hasn't, ask why and find out whether your town allows him to inspect after you've moved in. If it does not, then politely tell your developer that you'll come out to accept the property after the certificate of occupancy is issued. (After all, this procedure is intended to protect you and the rest of the community from unsafe and unhealthful construction.) If, as is probably the case, you may live in the new housing unit so long as inspection is made within a specified period, you should set a date to go and examine your new home.

At this point the builder's objective and yours are

diametrically opposite. He wants you to put your signature on paper accepting the housing unit so he can collect all the money due him. You want to make sure the place is in first rate condition and lives up to all those glowing descriptions in the builder's ads. You don't want to move into a home that is unfinished or one with major problems that will require workmen underfoot for lengthy changes/adjustments/ finishing. Remember, in this examination of your new home you have the upper hand in the form of that all-important signature of yours.

The builder may try to hustle you through the place. He may brush off your questions about incomplete work or unsatisfactory features with promises and a wave of the hand. Don't be rushed. He has everything to gain, you have much to lose. This is the time when you must carefully and systematically examine, test, try out all the promised features of your new home. That is why we recommend bringing along an expert. The plumbing, electric, air conditioning, heating, water heating systems, the doors and windows, floors and fixtures, extras such as fireplaces, trellises, and patios, etc., tile work and cabinetry, insulation, foundation, roof, and structural elements should be examined. Carefully.

Anything and everything not in working order or not as specified in the contract or purchase agreement should be noted in a list. If the bedroom window does not close properly, write that down. If the light switch or kitchen faucet or thermostat does not function right, note it. If the builder says his men will fix the flaws, ask when and write down the promised date beside each item. This will be your *list of exceptions*—an inventory of things that must be done before you will accept the unit.

RED FLAG: Do not sign anything whatsoever until you talk to your lawyer and discuss with him the list of changes to be made before the condominium is acceptable to you. You can, if urgently necessary, do it by telephone, but don't be stampeded into signing without referring to your lawyer. He will advise on the proper form for your "bill of exceptions" and your "acceptance" signature.

Example: With twenty-seven years of experience in the construction industry, a Rhode Island man moved into his new home in a development of $41,000 semi-attached units before all the final work was done. He made a careful inventory of problems and "work required" items and presented the list to the developer, who never got around to fixing any of them. One evening the new owner was sitting on his sofa in front of the fire when the brick facing on the floor-to-ceiling fireplace fell in a heap at his feet. He noticed that only 6 of the 104 bricks had been anchored to the wall. He then did what any of us would do: He called the builder.

The builder came around, cast a mournful eye at the pile of bricks. Words were exchanged, a lawsuit was mentioned, and the builder signed a promise to correct 80 items in the owner's list of exceptions. It shouldn't require a pile of bricks at your feet to get a builder to complete his work. But it might—if you sign first.

Keep these principles in mind:

1. If possible, don't accept your unit until necessary corrections have been made. Withholding your signature is the strongest bargaining weapon you have.

2. If possible, don't move in until major corrections have been completed. You may not wind up with a pile of bricks in your lap, but even the neatest of workmen can disrupt a home.

3. If you must move in before corrections are made, keep after the developer to take care of the "exceptions." Write down the dates by which he promises to complete the work. If the date(s) passes and the corrections have not been made, send a Xerox copy of the list of exceptions to the builder with a letter questioning why and requesting him to set a new date

for completion. Send the letter via certified mail, return receipt requested, so he'll know you mean business.

4. If the developer drags his feet and gives you copious excuses rather than satisfaction, take up the matter with your HOA. You probably are not the only owner who has corrections due from the builder. Get together with the others and present a master list of outstanding exceptions that must be taken care of by the developer. If he ignores this, legal action may be your only recourse.

6

Money Questions

The house was more covered with mortgages than with paint.

—George Ade

In this chapter we're going to look at some of the basics stemming from that one fundamental, money (or the lack of it). The elements we're going to cover are:

1. Whether to buy or rent.
2. Can you afford to buy?
3. Financing your purchase.
4. Shopping for the best deal on money.

Included under the second heading we have three examples of closing costs from widely disparate parts of the United States. If nothing else, you'll note from them the variety of things that may be part of the closing costs and the differences in such fees and charges. We caution you to look at these figures as indicators of the kinds of costs but not the actual amounts you may be charged.

1. *To buy or rent?* Usually the first question for young people who have never owned a house before is "Should I buy rather than rent?" The facts and figures on that are easily presented. Take houses or apartments that are essentially identical in size, features, and location. Assume, conservatively, that they will increase in value by at least a modest 4 percent per year. You can expect the landlord to take at least 10 percent profit each year (that's conservative

also). And property taxes plus maintenance costs should be reckoned at a minimum increase of 5 percent of the value of the house or apartment at the beginning of each year.

If we take a $40,000 property, here is a comparison of renting and buying. In this example the buyer put down $10,000 and took a twenty-five-year mortgage at 8.5 percent. Property taxes, maintenance, and insurance totaled 5.5 percent of the value of the house at the beginning of each year. A 10 percent return for the landlord is figured into the annual rent figures.

RENTING VS. BUYING

Year	Annual Rent	Annual Ownership Costs
1	$6,200	$6,960
2	6,448	4,965
3	6,706	4,303
4	6,974	3,975
5	7,253	3,780
6	7,543	3,652
7	7,845	3,561
8	8,159	3,495
9	8,485	3,444
10	8,824	3,404

As you can see, only in the first year does the renter come out ahead of the buyer. In fact, by the end of twenty-five years the rent will have grown to almost $16,000 per year—more than $1,300 a month. In the ten-year period, the renters will have paid $74,437 to their landlords and still have no equity in the property. The home buyers will have paid $41,539 and have a valuable stake in theirs. The renters will have paid $32,898 more than the buyers during the decade, or an average of $3,290 more per year. And at the end of twenty-five years the renters will have paid their landlords an average of $861 a month or $10,328 per year. The home buyer will have averaged $3,196 per year or $266 a month—that's about

two-thirds less than the renters' payout. To balance this example the renter should have the benefit of a $10,000 invest-
ment that's the down payment paid by the buyer in order to
purchase his house.

2. *Can you afford it?* O.K., you're convinced. You decide to
buy rather than rent. Can you afford it? Bankers generally use
a simple rule of thumb to get the answer: two and one-half
times your annual income is the amount you can afford to pay
for a home.

When it comes to the first of the month and the bills arrive,
your housing expense should total approximately one fourth of
your income. (Don't include overtime pay in your figures.)
That shelter total should include:

A. Mortgage payment—principal and interest.
B. Insurance.
C. Real estate taxes.
D. Heat and utilities.
E. Repairs, maintenance, and association dues.

FHA uses the "35–50 rule." FHA believes your total
housing expense usually should be 35% or less of your income
after federal taxes. This sum plus fixed obligations (payments
over one year term) should not exceed 50% of your income
after federal taxes.

There is some elasticity in these rules of thumb in both
directions. For instance, if you have heavy long-term expenses
such as illness in the family, a flock of youngsters or other
dependents, and have questionable job security, you'd better
buy a lower-priced home.

The repayment time is the other major elastic element in
the equation. The longer you take to pay off the mortgage, the
lower your monthly payments—but the greater your total
interest payments to the lender.

Texas real estate specialists recommend estimating your
monthly expenses this way:

A. Taxes—about 1.5 to 2 percent of market
price of house = $_____ ÷ 12 mos. = $_____

B. Insurance—homeowner's package @ .25 to 1 percent of market value = $_____ ÷ 12 mos. = $_____

C. Maintenance—estimated at 1.5 percent of market value = $_____ ÷ 12 mos. =   _____

D. Mortgage payments   _____

You can estimate payments on twenty-five- and thirty-year mortgages by consulting the chart below. Determine the interest rate and the term of the mortgage. Where the two intersect you will find the monthly dollar payment per $1,000 of mortgage. Simply multiply this figure by the number of thousands in your mortgage to find the total monthly mortgage payment.

HOME LOAN PAYMENT CALCULATOR
(Monthly principal + interest payments per $1,000 of mortgage)

Interest rate (%)	20 Years	25 Years	30 Years
7.5	$8.06	$7.39	$7.00
7.75	8.21	7.56	7.17
8	8.37	7.72	7.34
8.25	8.52	7.89	7.51
8.5	8.68	8.06	7.68
8.75	8.84	8.23	7.87
9	9.00	8.40	8.05
9.25	9.16	8.57	8.23
9.5	9.33	8.74	8.41

Example: If you have a gross income of $1,000 per month and you take out a 9 percent, thirty-year mortgage with a 10 percent down payment on the condominium, you can afford a mortgage of $24,300 on a value of $27,000. Your mortgage payment will be $8.05 × 24.3 (thousands) = $195.62. In Texas, the taxes, insurance, and upkeep would come to around $70 per month, for a total of about $266, just over the estimated fraction of your income earmarked for shelter. Obviously these costs vary widely in different parts of the nation. In Iowa, for instance, the total would be closer to $294.

If you are interested in figuring what your total interest payments will amount to over the entire term of the mortgage, you can use the chart above as follows: Multiply the monthly payments by the number of months in the term. Then subtract the original amount borrowed. The difference is the interest you will have paid over the full life of the loan. In our example above, the monthly payment ($195.62) × the months in the term (360) will equal the total paid: $70,423. Subtract the original amount borrowed ($24,300), and the remainder is the amount paid in interest: $46,123.

If any of this is unclear to you or you are unsure about it, go to your local bank or savings and loan association. They will usually be glad to help you with the figures. And they also will tell you what mortgage amount they are willing to lend you. After all, that's the real figure you should be using in your reckoning. But don't take the first figure you receive as the final one. (See the section in this chapter on shopping for money.)

What closing costs can you expect? (The "closing" is the meeting at which you turn over money and the seller turns over the deed and receipts for other elements of the purchase (oil in the tank, insurance, association dues, etc.).

Have the salesman put the closing costs in writing for you. On the next three pages are detailed examples from widely separated parts of the United States. They'll give you an idea of the wide differences in prices as well as variety of items included.

Experts in the Dallas area estimate that closing costs generally run between 3 and 4 percent of the price of the housing unit. (See page 100.)

In the Hawaiian example (page 101) the escrow agent is authorized to pay out in monthly installments construction costs for work completed as certified by either an architect or an engineer. The final payment is held until (*a*) the unit has been

DALLAS: CLOSING COSTS, $33,000 CONDOMINIUM, WITH $30,000 MORTGAGE

Items	Cost
Survey	$40
Title insurance (yours)	15
Escrow fee	15
Attorney fee (bank's)	65
Filing fee—county clerk	20
Restrictions and photos	10
Appraisal and credit report	75
Loan origination (1% of loan)	300
Interim interest (@ $7.90/day)	120
Prepaid Items	
Hazard insurance, 1 year	200
Hazard escrow, 2 months	35
Tax deposit, 2 months	100
Mortgage insurance (private co.)	150
TOTAL	$1,145

"substantially" completed and is ready for occupancy; (*b*) the developer advises the lender that the buyer has been notified that the unit is complete and ready for occupancy; and (*c*) the developer gives the lender evidence that the owner has accepted the unit.

These are helpful provisions that give the buyer added protection, for he may discover unfinished work in his final inspection of the unit. If he does, he may hold up the final payment until the corrections are satisfactorily completed.

The New York example (page 102) does not include prepayment of insurance and taxes, association and maintenance fees.

In each of these examples title insurance is mentioned. Many buyers of condominiums have title insurance on their units. Often the mortgage lender will require title insurance to protect his interest before he will make the loan. You pay

HAWAII: CLOSING COSTS, $34,000 CONDOMINIUM, WITH $30,600 MORTGAGE (and Loan Discount of 1½ Points)

Items	*Cost*
Recording fee	$14.50
Appraisal and credit report	46.50
Document preparation	17.00
Attorney fee (bank's)	30.00
Escrow fee	40.00
Title insurance (yours)	65.00
Recording mortgage	2.50
Mortgage service fee (1½% of loan)	459.00
Prepaid Items	
Mortgage insurance (private co.)	$153.00
Tax deposit, 3 months	119.00
Insurance, fire, liability; 1 yr.	62.40
Association dues, 2 mo.	10.50
Maintenance fee, 2 mo.	67.34
TOTAL	$1,086.74

the lender for this. If you pay a small additional premium you can buy title insurance to protect *your* interest. This coverage guarantees that your title is as stated in the public records. It also protects you from "hidden defects" in the deed or other documents.

A tremendous number of condominiums has been built in recent years under fifty different sets of state laws. Inevitably, some of the legal instruments drawn up may have discrepancies in them. In some cases these will create serious title problems for condominium purchasers. In fact, their titles may be invalid under the applicable state laws. Without thorough title investigation at the time of purchase, such buyers may not find out about their problems until they go to sell or refinance their units.

When you buy title insurance, the company's legal

NEW YORK: CLOSING COSTS, $60,000 TOWNHOUSE, WITH $40,000 MORTGAGE

Items	Cost
Survey	$100.00
Title insurance (yours)	165.00
Title research	25.00
Appraisal and credit report	107.50
Recording fee	8.50
Attorney fee (yours)	450.00
Attorney fee (bank's)	150.00
Title closer gratuity	10.00
Mortgage broker loan @ 2%	800.00
Prepaid Items	
Mortgage tax @ 1¼%	$500.00
Mortgage insurance	210.00
TOTAL	$2,526.00

specialists examine all the documents and, if they find them in order, issue a policy to you. If at any time thereafter your title is challenged, the policy insures you against any loss if the title is not as insured. And the title insurance company will defend your title in court if necessary. If the case is lost, the title insurance company is obligated to pay up to the full value of the policy.

RED FLAG: Since the policy will have been purchased at the time the property is bought, it will not cover any appreciation in value that may occur over the years.

Don't get carried away on this title insurance subject. In 99 cases out of 100 there may be no need for it. But then again, yours might be that one. (Robert Elliott, general counsel of the Department of Housing and Urban Development, estimates that of every $100 the title insurance companies receive in premiums, only slightly more than $1 is paid out in successful claims.)

In June 1975 a new federal law went into effect. It makes some changes that may save you money. Called the Real Estate Settlement Procedure Act, it prohibits kickbacks from title insurance companies to lawyers or banks, limits escrow requirements of lenders, and requires twelve days' advance disclosure of settlement costs for residential real estate.

According to Senator William Proxmire, using figures from a 1972 study by the Department of Housing and Urban Development, settlement costs average $2,816 (1974 prices). This is the national average of costs paid by both buyer and seller. These add up to a staggering total: $14 billion per year, nationwide.

The list of items that may be included in closing costs is as lengthy and assorted as an inventory of a bank's back room: fees to lawyers; surveyors; appraisers; for title search; credit report; termite inspection; preparation and recording of documents; title insurance; mortgage insurance; transfer taxes and broker's commissions. Also a closing fee for handling the settlement meeting itself; loan origination; for escrow; and mortgage discount points. And in addition there are prepaid items such as taxes and insurance premiums.

This new law requires that the mortgage lender give both seller and buyer a list of all settlement charges when he makes the loan commitment or no later than twelve days before the closing. One purpose of this is to make it possible for you to shop around for the best deal on all or any of the items included.

The prohibition on title insurance kickbacks should save you some money. It cuts out the 20 percent (average) "commission" that the title insurance companies generally give the person who refers the business to them. This is usually a lawyer or the mortgage bank. Some banks insist on selecting the title company before they will make a mortgage commitment. So for little more than a phone call they receive a "commission" from the title insurance company which comes out of your premium.

In another important provision, the new federal law limits

the amount of tax and insurance payments to be put in escrow to one month in advance. (Note the "prepaid" items in our examples above.) Senator William Brock, who sponsored this law, pointed out that many lenders required a buyer to pay as much as six months to two years of advance taxes and insurance premiums into the escrow account. Where this was the case, the new law makes it somewhat less costly for buyers.

One other benefit from title insurance: If the company refuses to insure your unit, it may be doing you a big favor. Its refusal will mean that something is wrong with the documents. It's far better that you know it before you put your money into the project than after.

In the New York closing example above, one of the expensive items not found in the Texas and Hawaii examples is the fee for your lawyer. It is one expense item that you can least afford to eliminate. If you think you can economize on some of the items listed, ask your banker or lawyer which ones.

The developer may present you with a nice, neat condominium package of contract and documents and copious assurances that there's not a thing to worry about.

That's true. There's not a thing for the developer to worry about. After all, his lawyers drew up the documents and he's looking out for himself, not you.

You need someone on your side, to look over the pages and pages of condolegalese. Don't make an expensive mistake by signing any agreement before an experienced real estate lawyer reviews the papers.

Your lawyer will analyze the title document to make sure you are indeed going to get what you think you are buying. He also will review the master deed and declaration setting up the condominium, and will determine that these are legal and registered with the proper authorities. He can check out the developer and officers of the development corporation to make sure their records are clear.

But those are not his only functions. He also should review

and approve: (1) the purchase agreement or contract; (2) reserves agreement; (3) insurance coverage; (4) by-laws of the homeowners' association outlining how the condominium will be governed; (5) the management contract; (6) the mortgage and all closing documents; (7) leases, if any.

We look at many of these essential matters in Chapter 9.

3. *Financing.* If you have the cash to buy a condominium unit outright, what are you doing reading this section? Skip it, you don't need it. In fact, if you have that kind of money, you probably don't need this book—you need a financial adviser.

If you don't have cash enough, you'll need help in financing your condominium purchase. That means, generally, securing a mortgage loan. There are two basic types:

A. Federal government insured—available through banks.

B. Conventional—available through banks, savings and loan institutions, insurance companies, mortgage companies, and often the developer.

The developer will usually tell you what financing is available on his units. That does not mean that you are limited to the mortgages he recommends. Check other sources.

Generally, low interest rate and small down payment will be the major advantages of government-insured mortgages. This is because the bank takes little risk when it loans money to a buyer under any of these. There are two basic federal government programs:

A. VA or GI loans, guaranteed by the Veterans Administration. These are available to all World War II and later vets.

B. FHA loans, insured by the Federal Housing Administration. Anyone may apply for an FHA loan. But he will have to be approved by the lender as a "good risk," and the housing unit he wishes to buy also will have to be appraised by one of its appraisers (and inspected by an FHA inspector if it is still to be built) before the FHA will sign the papers guaranteeing the mortgage.

FHA-insured mortgages have down payments that vary

depending on the size of the loan. On a $20,000 unit the minimum is $600 down; on a $25,000 unit the minimum is $750; and on $30,000 it is $1,250.

The required appraisal by an FHA inspector establishes the amount the FHA will guarantee. The VA has a similar procedure and issues a "Certificate of Reasonable Value" that tells its appraisal. In either case, the buyer may pay more than the appraised value, but it is up to him to find that additional money—which he will have to put into his down payment.

The interest rates on FHA and VA mortgages are set by the government. At present, the VA rate is a maximum of 8 percent. The FHA rate is now 8 percent plus 0.5 percent for FHA insurance: total, 8.5 percent. In addition, there are government subsidy programs available to those borrowers who qualify. The rates on these special loans are 7.75 percent in each case, plus 0.5 percent for FHA insurance. (Since these rates change without warning, you'll have to call your bank or the nearest FHA or VA office for the latest current figures.)

The VA and FHA programs set up useful financial regulations to protect consumers:

• Down payments must be put in escrow accounts and cannot be released to the developer until the unit is completed and title passes to the buyer.

• All planned construction must be complete.

• Units totaling 80 percent of the value of all units in the project must have been sold before FHA will guarantee any buyer's mortage.

• The buyer's title must be free and clear; it must be a first mortgage.

• The term of the mortgage may be as short as ten years and as long as thirty.

The mortgage may be no more than $45,000 (at this time). This limit may be changed by the FHA at any time; call your bank for the latest figure. There are other stipulations limiting the amount available. For instance, if the purchase is by a buyer who will not be occupying the unit, he may expect a maximum of only 85 percent of the amount available to a buyer who will be living in his own unit.

On completion of a condominium project, the FHA requires from the developer legal, fair, and equitable agreements covering vital aspects of condominium transactions and life in them. Among other things: (*a*) evidence of zoning compliance; (*b*) surety bond against latent defects equal to 2.5 percent of total mortgage; (*c*) regulatory agreement—which provides for reserves for maintenance and replacement of worn-out roofs, equipment, etc., sets out how assessments and collections shall be made, how defaults will be handled, how upkeep, record-keeping, and reporting are to be done, and prevents remodeling or changes without FHA approval.

As this is written, the construction industry is in one of its worst slumps since the Great Depression. It is building fewer housing units and having trouble selling them because tight money has made banks and other lenders reluctant to put out mortgage money. In many cases the lending institution will charge top interest and require as much as 50 percent down. VA- and FHA-backed loans are extremely attractive—to the borrower—by comparison. For lending institutions, however, they may give little profit. They are, therefore, unpopular with lenders. That and the red tape associated with these government-backed loans currently keep the FHA-insured proportion of the mortgage market to less than 5 percent of new housing.

The vast bulk of mortgage loans is made by banks and savings and loan institutions. The interest rates and down payments required vary considerably. In general, the rate will be higher than the FHA/VA loan rates, and there is likely to be an additional fee of 1 percent of the total as an "origination" fee to the lender. Builders may be able to offer more attractive terms than these. The closest approach to such low-down-payment mortgages in the nongovernmental sector are those insured by private mortgage insurance companies such as MGIC (called "Magic" by bankers). MGIC is the Mortgage Guarantee Insurance Corporation. It acts in a manner similar to FHA and VA, but for profit.

You initiate the MGIC participation by asking your lender to give you the particulars on a mortgage with and without private mortgage insurance. In general, you'll find that the privately insured mortgage will require a lower down payment than conventional mortgages—as little as 5 or 10 percent in some cases. However, it will cost 1 to 3 percent more. (The insurance company adds its fee to the bank's.)

The private insurance company's experts review the complete condominium project package before they approve it for their participation. The fact that it has met the insurance company's criteria for marketability and resale is an endorsement of the project. That should make it easier to resell the unit later.

4. *Shop for money.* In the free market for housing and for mortgage money, it pays to shop around. Even in the current credit crunch, there are some places in the nation where the oversupply of condominiums has caused developers—at least temporarily—to take unusual steps to sell their products.

One condominium project, Aptucxet Village in Massachusetts, is beckoning buyers by offering a free twenty-five-inch color TV set to purchasers. And it has arranged mortgage financing at an unusually favorable 8.75 percent rate.

Another Massachusetts project, Dennis Bayside Condominiums, is competing on the basis of cost. The developer has arranged mortgages with a down payment of only 20 percent (relatively low in this area at this time) and an interest rate of 8 percent. Beyond those two features, he has made arrangements for second-step financing in order to attract current homeowners. If you buy one of the condominium units and have a home anywhere in the state, you will be assisted in selling it by lenders who have agreed to provide a mortgage to the buyers of your house. Of course the buyers have to be financially qualified, but in tight-money times such as these, even the qualified frequently cannot find a lender at the necessary moment. This farsighted arrangement on the part of the developer helps overcome that hazard and helps his prospects sell their homes in order to buy his condominiums.

In California, one developer offered an extraordinary year-end 1974 deal to buyers. Las Brisas, a condominium development in Anaheim, offered a free auto, a motorboat, or a $2,500 down-payment credit to buyers of units selling for $29,950 to $36,950, if they bought before the end of 1974!

Perhaps in your section of the nation the real estate situation is quite different. You may be in a sellers' market. In any case, spend some time and energy seeking the best deal on a mortgage. In the long run you may save thousands.

Don't end your mortgage-money search unless you're satisfied that you can't get a VA or FHA mortgage. If not, then try for a conventional mortgage from:

A. Commercial banks
B. Savings banks
C. Savings and loan associations
D. Insurance companies
E. Private mortgage money companies
F. Your lodge, fraternal organization, union, or credit union

And don't forget to try at least one additional bank—you may find a substantial difference in rates or closing costs by shopping around.

7

Resort/Vacation Condominiums

There was too much scenery and fresh air. What I need is a steam-heated flat with no ventilation or exercise.

—O. HENRY

Resort or vacation condominiums have extraordinary financial advantages, in addition to their obvious attractions as second homes or holiday havens. They offer many if not all the advantages of conventional condominiums, as well as:

1. Income from rental
2. Additional tax deductions for:
   A. Maintenance and repairs
   B. Operating expenses
   C. Depreciation on property and furnishings
   D. One or more inspection visits to your property annually
   E. Management fees, brokerage, agency fees, commissions on rental property
   F. Insurance premiums—fire, casualty

Resort condominiums are often (though not always) attached townhouse units, usually designed and decorated in a style suitable to the setting—stucco and Spanish tiles in

California, Georgian porticos and ante-bellum colonnades in Georgia and Florida, Alpine fretwork, wood siding, and "cuckoo clock" balconies in Vermont and Colorado ski chalets. In resort areas where land has become scarce, such as Miami Beach, Spain's Costa del Sol, and Mexico's Acapulco, condominiums are often in high-rise buildings.

Condominiums in such chic sunneries as the Aga' Khan's Costa Smeralda in Sardinia, the Marbella Club in Spain, and the Tryall Estate Club at Montego Bay, Jamaica, have long attracted moneyed international travelers. But only in recent years have American investors realized the possibilities of such second-home opportunities in the United States.

Resort condominium ads often follow the "promise her anything" premise—and some actually deliver. The ads are skillful exercises in advertising jargon laced with legalese. You're likely to be enticed with offers that promise the "use of lakes, swimming pool, shuffleboard, country club, tennis courts, free bus service, as well as reduced rates for motel, greens fees, and country-club-sponsored forms of entertainment." It sounds lush, and the fine print may gloss over the cost of such benefits, but you can jolly well bet the fine print of the sales contract states ever so clearly (if you can read three-point type) that many of the promises are really extras, available for an unspecified fee.

Some ads even offer to help you sell your present home, but the fine print isn't quite so specific about how *much* help you'll actually get. "Our professional staff will advise you on what to do with your home to make it salable and will advise the people buying your home on how to get a mortgage." Big deal.

As in all condominium offerings, you will want to review carefully the public offering statement, contract, declaration, budget, survey, by-laws, board/committees, and management agreement for the resort/vacation development you're considering.

Since the decision to buy a resort condominium is generally based not only on your own exclusive use of the place but on its rental potential, it should be examined accordingly. This means that you should look at your purchase as an investment as well as a second home. If you are not equipped to evaluate investment potential, you'll want to confer with trusted professionals on these matters. We suggest talking with your accountant or tax adviser, your lawyer, and your banker.

But there are additional factors involved in resort/vacation condominiums. Among them, these are worth examining in depth:

1. *Recreation facilities.* Since these may be the major attraction in your resort condominium purchase, you'll certainly want to ask basic questions such as: (*a*) Are these facilities available to you without further charge? (*b*) Are they leased or owned by the condominium complex? (*c*) If leased, can fees be boosted without owners' approval? (*d*) If you rent out your unit, can your tenants use the facilities without extra charge?

If you are buying from the plans and sketches because the project is incomplete or still to be built, the feasibility study and analysis of competition are of paramount importance. In these you will find the experts' appraisals of the project from the standpoint of its facilities and amenities and its possibilities as a moneymaker. The information in these studies should be factual, specific, up to date, and logical.

2. *The project itself.* Resort and vacation condominiums are often purposely located in areas more or less remote from cities. When this is the case, you as a prospective buyer must be on guard about potential problems such as these:

A. Access roads, streets, and street lighting—who installs and maintains these? What will your maintenance costs be?

B. Utilities and sewer lines—who pays for these installations? How can you be sure that they are adequate for the condominium population projected? (There must be engineering surveys and feasibility studies of these matters. Ask to see them.)

C. Safe water—a matter of increasing concern. What will be the source of potable water for the condominium? Will it be (a) sufficient and (b) safe, both now and in the future? What assurance do you have other than the developer's verbal promise? If this is a condominium that depends greatly on waterfront for its appeal, what is the pollution profile of that water now? And what is the projected pollution prediction for five and ten years hence? The health department of the government jurisdiction you are in may have valuable information on this if the developer does not. Often you may find that the state health department and/or public health school of your state university can help on these matters. Even such famed beaches as the Riviera at St. Tropez in France have been closed down at times because of pollution.

D. Building code. Maybe there is none for the area in which this development is located. All the more reason to go over the construction carefully, or have someone seasoned in building do so.

> Sometimes ye olde logge cabin looketh quaint,
> But because it concealeth short cuts, sound construction
>   it ain't.

The same may be true regardless of the type of construction. So much depends on the builder and his reputation for integrity.

E. Fire safety. Out in the boondocks you're more than somewhat vulnerable. Find out for certain what the fire protection facilities are. You may discover that the only fire fighters are the condominium's office and maintenance crews. Check built-in fire warning and fire escape mechanisms at the project itself.

F. Remoteness. Many resort/vacation condominiums are purposely remote. That sometimes causes certain problems. For instance, is there any zoning in the area? If not, will your view or access to the major features of the area (ski slopes, shoreline, and so on) be endangered by future building, by either this or some other developer? What about public transportation to the site? Does it exist? If not, will it be extended there? This can be a valuable plus in renting. Is the project's isolation a possible hazard to someone with a health problem? How remote from good health facilities are you? Can they be reached fast in an emergency?

G. Security. What about the overall security of the project? Any reason to fear vandalism, theft, or other crime? What police protection is available? How about security against natural hazards such as avalanches, floods, hurricanes? Are both the project and you covered by protective barriers and/or construction? What would such a catastrophe do to your investment? What will insurance for your individual unit cost?

Most, if not all, of these questions are answered in full disclosures to be found in the SEC prospectus and others of its type.

3. *SEC Registration/SEC Prospectus.* As we outlined in Chapter 5, recreation condominiums sold as investments in interstate commerce in the United States are required to register with the Security and Exchange Commission (SEC). They must file an offering document called a prospectus. Among the additional information you will find in the prospectus filed with the SEC will be a discussion of competition that your resort condominium can expect; rates that will be charged renters; fees for management services and what these cover; times you may use your unit and costs assessed you (if any) for doing so; the advertising and promotional plans for the resort; the professional background and experience of those who will manage the project; and much more, including the names, addresses, and investment of the principal holders of interests in the project.

Don't look for promises of any specific return on your purchase price. SEC regulations prohibit any such claims. Even the salesman may be extremely reluctant to give any estimates on this, for he, too, is forbidden to make such statements.

If the project you're considering is not registered with the SEC, it may be worthwhile to ask, "Why not?" and to pursue the answer a bit further.

Keep in mind, however, that SEC registration does *not* mean that the SEC has approved the project. It merely means that the developer has met the letter of the law that requires registering an offering. His statements in it must be factual, else he's liable to prosecution for a federal offense. But he may indicate in the prospectus that it's an investment not likely to succeed, or that its management fees are exorbitant or its amenities minimal—all stated in language that may be elliptical enough to escape the casual or uninformed reader. (One more good reason for having an experienced lawyer by your side.)

4. *Management.* Because income from rental is an important factor in deciding whether to buy or not to buy, you'll want to remember that for success in this matter you need all the help you can get. You are buying not only the appeals and amenities of the project, you are also buying management skills. Therefore, study with care the management contract and/or the background and experience of the managers and their discussion of the way the rental operation will be conducted. To evaluate all of this you need to call on your banker or accountant. Perhaps you need a Dun and Bradstreet report on the management organization; your banker can order one.

Examine closely the powers of unit owners. Chances are that you will find the developer or management organization has a majority of votes in the owners' association. Don't be surprised: they want to make sure they control the operation without the danger of some unit owners' revolt that might overturn their entire operation. There is probably not a thing you can or should do about this matter, but be aware of it before you sign on the dotted line.

5. *Rental income.* In general, here's how it works: You buy a unit in a ski complex at Vail, Colorado, because you like to ski and love the climate and stunning beauty of the area. Furthermore, the agent for the condominium complex explains that you can collect income on your unit when you're not using it. Since you live more than a thousand miles away and can't possibly use the unit except on long weekends or vacations, this possibility is what tips the balance in favor of your purchase.

Management asks you to sign a contract appointing them rental agents and spelling out their duties and responsibilities, what you can expect in fees, services, and charges, and what use you may expect to make of the unit. Generally, the management organization is the rental agent. The contract between you itemizes the specific furnishings the unit will have, down to the number of knives, forks, trivets, and towels. This makes certain that all the units will have uniform equipment and furnishings so they can be rented out on a businesslike basis.

The rental agent wants your property to be available for as much of the year (and especially the peak season) as possible. Usually your contract will call for a maximum of forty-six weeks of rental use and the remaining six weeks for your use, specifying the dates you intend to enjoy it. Since peak season rates are the highest, you may forgo using the unit during that time in order to bring in the highest return in rent. But the choice is up to you.

The agent then advertises the entire complex as one great resort. Renters are actually more like hotel guests, and there is a hotel desk functioning on an around-the-clock basis to give guests all the services one would expect in a resort hotel. Daily maid service is provided, as are linens, laundry, cleaning, repairs and upkeep of buildings, grounds, recreational facilities, garage and parking spaces, roads and sidewalks, reception desk, and mail and telephone service. All these are management responsibilities, typical of first-rate hotel services.

The management is responsible for your property. Therefore it requires a deposit from renters. When they check out, an inspection is made to determine if all is well with your unit or if a chunk of the deposit must be retained to cover damage. Management then cleans your unit. Your rental income is credited to your account and sent to you at prearranged times. For its services, the management agency receives a fee, ranging from 15 to 50 percent of rental income.

There are infinite variations on this general scheme. The major variation is the "rental pool," in which the rentals from your unit and all others in the complex are merged into a "pool." At the end of the year all money in the pool is divvied up according to a formula stated in your deed or agreement. Usually it is based on the cost of each unit in the entire resort. Management's fees and maintenance assessments come out of the pool before you receive yours, of course.

6. *Tax benefits.* Tax laws are here today, gone tomorrow. The following information is based on the laws current at this writing. Be sure to check with your tax specialist as to whether they are still in force when you read this—and what is more important, how they apply to you. Basic information will be found in Internal Revenue Service publications No. 527, *Rental Income and Royalty Income,* and No. 534, *Tax Information on Depreciation.*

The tax benefits of a so-called tax shelter are those written into the federal tax code to aid businessmen. They apply to a resort condominium only to the extent that it is a business venture. And since when have you been in the resort business? Only since you began renting your condominium unit when you weren't using it.

Tax regulations that give you tax shelter advantages apply only during the period of time that you have the property up for rental. On that portion of the year you will be able to deduct business costs. So if you occupy your unit one month out of twelve and rent it the rest of the year, you are a landlord for eleven-twelfths of the year. Once you establish that the condominium was purchased as an investment, you will be able to deduct up to eleven-twelfths of your expenses for insurance, management fees, commissions, maintenance and repairs, operating expenses, and depreciation of property and furnishings. In addition, you will be able to deduct real estate taxes and mortgage interest (as in normal home ownership) and the documented cost of one or more inspection trips to your property. Just how much benefit you will derive from all this depends on the amount you spend and your income bracket. Obviously the benefits *can be* substantial, especially at tax time.

7. *Depreciation.* This is one tax shelter benefit that deserves greater explanation. Depreciation applies to the building portion of your condominium unit and to its furnishings. The IRS may estimate the useful life of your condominium at twenty years. Normally, therefore, your depreciation would be one-twentieth of the price of the building each year for twenty years. This is called straight-line deduction.

It is possible, however, to write down the depreciation at a faster rate. If your condominium is new, residential, and rented out for income purposes, you may be able to take a depreciation deduction at twice the straight-line rate on the portion of the year the unit is up for rent. Here is how it works out for a new $20,000 resort condominium:

Cost of condominium
(excluding cost of land): $20,000

Useful life: 20 years

Annual depreciation,
straight-line method: $\dfrac{\$20,000}{20\ \text{years}} = \$1,000$ per year

200 percent basis: $1,000 \times 200\% = \$2,000$ per year

However, you may deduct depreciation only for the portion of the year you had the unit up for rent, that is, eleven of the twelve months, so your figures would be: $11/12 \times \$2,000 = \$1,833$ per year. This would be the total depreciation allowable for your first year.

Before figuring the second year's depreciation, that taken the first year must be subtracted:

$$\$20,000 - \$1,833 = \$18,167.$$

This is how your deductions for depreciation would look for the first five years:

Year no. 1:	$1,833
2:	1,666
3:	1,513
4:	1,374
5:	1,248
TOTAL:	$7,634

Obviously there is a considerable cash benefit in the form of usable income liberated by this system of reckoning depreciation and deducting it on your income tax return. Don't lose track, however, of the fact that this accelerated depreciation in the early years balances out in the later years. In the last five years of the building's twenty-year life you will have relatively little depreciation to write off. Your financial situation may have changed by then, and if you have retired and are living on a smaller income your tax bracket may have shifted downward sufficiently so that you won't need large depreciation deductions then as much as you do now.

Another depreciation factor you may use is the amount available from furniture and furnishings of your rental condominium. IRS estimates that these have a life of ten years and straight-line depreciation must be used on them. If you have $4,000 worth of furnishings in your unit, your depreciation might look like this:

Cost of furnishings	$4,000
Salvage value (10%)	−400
Value available	$3,600

Annual depreciation, straight-line method:
$$\frac{\$3,600}{10 \text{ years}} = \$360 \text{ per year}$$
Annual depreciation allowable:
$$\$360 \times 11/12 \text{ year} = \$330 \text{ per year}$$

In summary, here is how your deductibles might add up on a $20,000 resort condominium (excluding land cost) in the first year:

Depreciation, building	$1,833
Depreciation, furnishings	330
Property taxes, annual (estimated)	500
Expenses, round-trip, to inspect property	300
Maintenance, including insurance and repairs	550
Rental expenses, fees, and commissions	800
Mortgage interest	1,200
TOTAL	$5,513

From this total you would have to deduct any rental income received. If it amounts to $2,000 for the year, your total deductibles would be $5,513 − $2,000 rental income = $3,513 net "loss."

If you establish the fact that you purchased the property as an investment, if you are not retired and are in the 35 percent income tax bracket, you may derive a tax benefit of as much as

$1,230, in addition to the rental income of $2,000. So your total benefit would be $3,230 for the first year.

We have dwelt at length on the financial advantages of resort condominiums for these are often the essential, hard-headed factors that help you decide whether to buy or not to buy.

To give you some idea of the kind of report you may expect if you buy a resort condominium that operates on the pool principle, we have an example (below). This is a typical annual fiscal report, sent to each unit owner by the management company. Note that it includes unitemized expenses and taxes. Management charges 20 percent of gross for its services. The units sell at prices from $42,500 to $135,000, and there are 407 of them. Our example is one of the minimum-priced units, entitled to .33 percent of the profits or deficit. You will find that our unit received a cash distribution of $1,400 earlier in the year and $633 as a year-end payout for a total of $2,033 for the year or 4.8 percent on the investment of $42,500.

FISCAL YEAR ENDED JULY 31, 1974

Share of Operating Income

1.	Total gross unit revenues	$3,000,000
2.	Share due to Unit #____	10,000
3.	Percentage of Item 2 to Item 1	.33%
4.	Operating income for fiscal year	1,000,000
5.	Share of operating income due Unit #____ (Item 3 × Item 4)	$ 3,333

Capital Account, Unit #____

6.	Capital account of Unit #____ at start of fiscal year	$ 300
7.	Add: Share of operating income for year	3,333
		$3,633

8. Less: Expenses during fiscal year,
   Unit #_____ $ 800
   Property taxes paid fiscal
   year, Unit #_____   400
   Interim cash distributions,
   Unit #_____   1,400

        −2,600 $2,600

9. Capital account, prior to year-end
   distribution $1,033

10. Year-end capital account (% in-
    terest in common elements of Unit
    #_____ × aggregate capital ac-
    counts of all partners after year-
    end distribution)   400

         $ 633

11. Excess (Item 9 less Item 10) dis-
    tributed herewith $ 633

12. Deficit (Item 10 less Item 9) to be
    repaid to partnership   none

As we have pointed out earlier, there are substantial benefits in addition to rental income that owners may expect from their resort units. These include use of the vacation facility plus tax benefits. For our resort condominium example, these are typical benefits during one year's operation:

1. 28 (or more) days' vacation use of unit at a saving over retail (owners are charged minimum fee for linen and maid service), depending on season and unit, from $475 to $1,475

2. Tax benefits, excluding owner's use of unit
   a. Expense of annual trip to inspect property   350

b. Depreciation (new units, based on
   33-year useful life and 150% rate)   1,970
c. Property taxes   400
d. Interest @ 8¼% average for first five
   years on mortgage on 75% of pur-
   chase price   2,690
e. Management fees   1,737
f. Maintenance   expenses,   common
   elements   846
                                               _____
   TOTAL TAX BENEFITS $7,993
3. Potential benefits
   (Item 1 plus item 2): $8,468 to $9,468

8

Resales:
Bargain Condominiums?

Property is necessary, but it is not necessary that it
should remain forever in the same hands.
—RÉMY DE GOURMONT

A few years ago a chapter such as this would have been
unnecessary. But today, with millions of Americans living in
condominiums, there may be thousands of resale units on the
market.

On the key question, are resale condominiums a good or a
bad deal? we can state boldly and without equivocation, that
depends. Let's have a look.

1. *Advantages.* First off, you can secure *solid information*
on financial matters that can only be *estimated* on a newly
built condominium. The taxes are a matter of record, as are
the operating and maintenance charges, assessments for
reserves and emergencies, and the insurance costs and extras
necessary, whether for garbage collection or leaf disposal.

Second, the problems that may afflict a new condominium
project probably have been worked out by the time of a resale.
The leaky roof or noisy heating system, the structural,
landscape, or architectural problems will have been
corrected—one hopes. Human behavior problems also may
have straightened out. The people who simply cannot
function in a cooperative, interdependent community will

have moved out. The homeowners' association will have developed an effective board of directors and have found an efficient management team to run the project (or so one hopes).

Third, the intrinsic value of the resale unit may be higher than that of those built later. Such elements as higher ceilings, superior materials, more closets, and larger rooms are examples. So, too, the location might be more choice than on a newly built project. Resale units may have better views, be closer to the beach/golf/recreation facilities and public transportation, shops, and so on.

Fourth, the resale unit may offer the chance to secure a mortgage at a lower rate than the prevailing market offers. You may be able to take over the existing mortgage. If its rate is 7 percent and the current market rate is 10 percent, you'll save thousands of dollars in interest payments.

2. *Disadvantages or problem areas.* Keep in mind above all that buying a used condominium is different in some fundamental ways from purchasing a single-family house. As we have pointed out, the condominium buyer is joining an organization or kind of a family/community. You'll want to look over this "family" very carefully before joining it.

You'll also want to check out very carefully the unit you're considering. The experts warn that condominium resales are almost unregulated but have all the inherent risks of purchasing from the developer directly, plus many additional, potentially costly risks as well.

As one condominium specialist points out, in a *new* project the buyer has the benefit of state laws and the public offering statement, declaration, survey, and by-laws to guide him and the state laws to help protect him. But in a *resale*, there is no requirement of full disclosure or penalties imposed on the seller as in an original sale. An exception, at this point, is the state of Virginia, which has taken a pioneering step forward, as we shall see.

Another sobering question for the prospective buyer

should be: Would I give $20,000 (or whatever the purchase price may be) to buy into a company if I didn't know:

A. Its financial condition. How much does it owe? When are its debts coming due? What is its income?

B. What are its assets? What are its liabilities?

C. Does it have any lawsuits outstanding? Any claims or liens? Any judgments against it?

D. Does it owe back taxes? Are its taxes about to increase?

E. How has it been run? Has it been profitable? What is the record of the current management?

F. What is the condition of its physical plant? Are the buildings in good repair? How about the land and grounds? How about equipment, such as maintenance machinery and vehicles?

It may seem farfetched to bring up questions such as these when you're thinking about buying housing. But whether you like it or not, that resale condominium you're considering is part of a going business—a sizable one. And if you don't dig beneath the surface, you may buy yourself a peck of trouble. That nice guy who is selling his condominium to you just may have a substantial bill with the HOA for unpaid assessments, taxes, and special charges. If you buy, the unit's debts become yours.

Here are a few suggestions to help you find out as much as you can about a resale unit before you buy it.

First, ask the seller for the documents we mention in this section. They will help you evaluate the condominium project as it was originally conceived, the HOA as it was set up, the budgeted costs as projected, and the management responsibilities as outlined in the contract.

Second, get from the seller information on the current status of (*a*) the entire project and (*b*) his specific unit. These are the data you're after:

A. A "recordable statement," i.e., a notarized, legal document stating the amount of unpaid assessments, taxes, special levies, and all other money owed the HOA on the unit being offered for sale. This statement should come from an officer of the HOA. What you want is an official spellout of what is due and outstanding on the unit. You should then deduct the total due from the price you'll pay the seller (because these are his obligations).

B. The declaration and by-laws of the project. What you want to peruse is the clause called "Restraints on Alienation." This is the one that requires "first refusal" by the HOA on any resale. If this clause is operative, get a statement in writing from an HOA officer that the HOA will approve sale to you.

C. Capital expenditures scheduled by the HOA this year and in the future; the amount of reserves in the replacement fund; and the amount of these reserves earmarked for the capital expenditures scheduled. Get this statement in writing from an officer of the HOA. The purpose of this is to let you know what major cash outlays are scheduled, and how many of them may be covered by existing reserves. The difference will be the amount you'll have to help pay as an owner.

D. Current financial statement (or the most recent monthly, quarterly, or annual report) of the HOA. If it doesn't have one, consider this a *Red Flag* and proceed with extreme caution. The financial statement should give the figures for regular assessment income, expenses, fees, reserves, special assessments, taxes, and so on. This will help you determine whether the financial condition of the condominium complex is healthy or near bankruptcy. You'll also be able to see directly what your monthly payments will be and to what purposes they will go.

E. Copies of the master insurance policies—casualty and liability especially, as well as the policy(s) covering the individual unit you're considering. The master policies should be written, as we shall explain further in Chapter 9, so as to cover replacement costs of the buildings and equipment. If the policies are dated several years back, chances are they seriously undervalue the buildings because inflation has caused values to soar. Question this.

RED FLAG: A matter of special concern should be the liability coverage.

Example: In a midwestern high-rise condominium, the HOA reduced liability coverage during an economy drive. Several months later an elevator accident severely injured one of the residents. The claim for personal injury damages was far in excess of the policy limits. If the actual figure allowed by the courts also exceeds these limits, the difference will be charged to unit owners.

F. Current management contract. Ask to see this. Purpose: the contract spells out the manager's responsibilities and pay. It also will be dated. If the date is recent, ask questions: Why has a new manager been hired? What happened to the previous manager? Who was he? (Maybe you should try to contact him and discuss the condominium with him, keeping in perspective his possible reasons for prejudice.) How many managers has the project had since it was opened? If there have been many, why? Does the contract cover the requirements of such a condominium? Those requirements are basically three: running a community, managing its finances, and carrying out its legal obligations. (See Chapter 9 for details.) It's a rare person who can accurately evaluate a contract designed to guarantee delivery on all three counts. We suggest you confer with the real estate specialists at your local bank or trust company—preferably persons familiar with real estate management.

It's not easy to determine whether the manager is knowledgeable in tax and real estate law, but obviously he should be. He'll have to deal with Internal Revenue Service regulations as well as state and local tax laws. He'll have to operate the condominium under the state's horizontal property act provisions. He'll have to be familiar with insurance matters and will have to see that coverage is adequate but not exorbitant. He must be versed in rating the life expectancy of materials and equipment, from roof shingles to basement boilers, in order to calculate reserve requirements for common elements of the project. And he must know his stuff when it comes to maintenance of grounds, recreational facilities, equipment, and managing the necessary crews.

G. The most recent assessment statement for the unit you're considering. Secure a copy to be sure you know about any hidden or forgotten expenses you'll be dunned for. Does the statement include garbage disposal, yard and common element services, seasonal work such as screens or storm window installation and removal? In other words, what extras can you expect beyond the monthly maintenance/operations charges? You also need clear-cut, reliable evidence of the services, amenities, and privileges provided by the HOA. Is a parking space assigned? If so, where? Do you have automatic entry to the pool, tennis courts, and the rest, or must you join a club, pay dues and use fees? Or are the facilities leased, with the annual fees escalating each year?

Virginia's new condominium law is the first to help protect a buyer of a resale unit. The Virginia statute places on the individual seller the same penalties for false, deceptive, or misleading advertising, promotional, or sales methods as upon a professional real estate developer or his agents. Furthermore, the law makes the seller responsible for furnishing to you, the buyer, an official statement from the HOA about the unpaid assessments on his unit (if any), and any by-law restrictions on his right to sell to you. The seller is also responsible for a capital expenditures' schedule and for a statement on status of reserves and current and scheduled payouts from the reserves for any purpose. These he must furnish you. This Virginia law specifies that the "principal officer" of the HOA must furnish these statements upon written request within ten days. That makes it impossible for the seller to stall with the alibi that he has not been able to get the necessary papers from the HOA.

In addition to these important papers, you'll want to go on a careful, detailed walkabout inspection. Take the guided tour. Examine the common elements. Are they in good condition? Is it obvious that they've been kept up, that the grounds and facilities are well maintained? Or is deterioration obvious to the point that repairs and replacements are imminent? If you're not expert at judging such matters, take along a friend who knows something about building upkeep, real estate, appraisals, and the like. Your inspection tour will tell you something about the current assessments of the HOA. Of course assessments can be kept low—if corners are cut on maintenance. But the day of reckoning finally comes with a bang!

Finally, don't make this purchase a do-it-yourself job. It is even more important that you have professional assistance in buying a condominium resale than in buying from the original seller. We've tried to highlight some of the problem areas, but our brief list by no means exhausts the possibilities. Just remember that even though it may appear clear-cut, a condominium resale can be more complicated by far than the usual single-family house purchase.

9

Condominium Fundamentals

> One of the greatest pieces of economic wisdom is
> to know what you do not know.
> —JOHN KENNETH GALBRAITH

This is a nuts and bolts chapter. In it you will find the basic elements you should be aware of and background information about the documents you may face in your search for a condominium home.

Throughout, our approach to the promises of condominium advertising, promotion, and salesmen is one of skepticism. Not that we believe all developers and their agents are by nature deceitful and larcenous. Far from it. Without the developer and his entrepreneurial enterprise there would be no condominiums for you to consider. Anyone who takes on the complicated task of building and marketing housing in these United States deserves praise and thanks as well as a reasonable profit.

We trust that the vast majority of condominium developers are upright and honest businessmen. But, as they say about playing cards around the family table, "Sure you trust your mother, but cut the cards." This chapter is written in that spirit. You'll find few references to the ways in which developers have acted like beneficent angels, and many to ways developers have taken advantage. The reason for this imbalance is simple: We—and you as a prospective buyer—have a right to expect developers/sellers to act ethically and fulfill their commitments. In other words, you don't need to be protected from sellers who act honestly. You don't need to be warned against ethical behavior. It is your right to expect it. We're here to help you with the unexpected—the short cuts, ploys, and stratagems that you might not anticipate and would not look for without a bit of guidance.

So in the pages that follow we'll highlight factors that bear close attention. This material is not easy going—it's technical and dry, but it covers the central provisions that may determine whether your condominium hunt is a success or a disaster. Remember, these pages are no substitute for professional help from your banker, accountant, tax adviser, and lawyer. But these pages will have served their purpose if they alert you to pitfalls and shortcomings in the condominium offerings you're considering.

Here is our agenda for this chapter:

1. *Public offering statement* or *prospectus*—the naked truth (?) about project and developer.

2. *Contract* or *purchase agreement*—what it contains: description, price, deposit and escrow, title, HOA, your voting power, cancellation rights, cooling-off period.

3. *Declaration* or *master deed*—birth certificate, private, limited, and common elements, owner no-nos, recreation and other facilities, leases, cost/expenses, homeowners' association (HOA), restrictions on owners, phase construction.

4. *Budget*—a sample; monthly charges—for what?; low-balling.

5. *Survey and plans*—cubes of title, "as-built" drawings, layouts, and elevations.

6. *By-laws*—the constitution and working rules of the condomocracy; owner self-government, developer phase-out, vetos, leases, warranties, three Rs, HOA powers, owner responsibilities, fees and assessments, standards of service, reserves, insurance, amendments.

7. *Board and committees*—who does what; handbook.

8. *Management agreement*—duties and responsibilities of the manager.

1. *Public offering statement (also called prospectus and disclosure document).* The most effective protection of condominium buyer interests is achieved in those states that demand, by law, that the truth be told to possible buyers and which put teeth in that law.

Virginia's new condominium law socks it to developers and their agents and even individuals reselling their own condominium units who "willfully" make untrue statements or omit material facts. These are misdemeanors, and if found guilty, the seller may be fined not less than $1,000 or twice the amount of gain from the sale, whichever is larger, up to a limit of $50,000. He can be sent to jail for up to six months as well, or instead of the fine, for each offense.

Because of this tough stance, a public offering statement from a Virginia condominium project is likely to be reliable and complete in its description and factual material. It is likely to be more so than such a statement from a state where the laws are lax.

The public offering statement is supposed to give prospective buyers full and accurate information about the condominium development and its units. It should tell all, including unusual circumstances or features that affect the condominium.

Here is what you may expect to find in the better public offering statements or prospectuses:

A. Name and address of both the condominium and the developer.

B. General description of the project, telling the number of units, number to be sold and rented, number to be included in future expansion, if any. (This last point is important; under Section 3, Declaration, see the portion about "phase construction.")

C. The texts of both declaration and by-laws, information about developer's control of the condominium, a projected budget covering at least the first year of operation, with a breakdown of expenses for each unit and assessments for reserves. Also, any restrictive covenants limiting resale of the units by owners.

D. Copies of management contract, any lease of facilities or agreement affecting your use or access to any part of the project. The effect of each such agreement on the purchaser should be spelled out. And the relationship, if any, between the developer, the managing agent, and the restrictive agreement should be stated.

E. Evidence of compliance with state or local ordinances, regulations, building permits, zoning, and site plan approvals.

F. List of any encumbrances, liens, etc., affecting title.

G. Terms of financing offered by developer to unit buyers.

H. Warranties by the developer on the units and common areas over and beyond what is stated in by-laws.

I. Cancellation clause, giving buyer ten days after receipt of the current public offering statement or contract date, whichever is later.

In addition, Virginia law requires that the developer not alter the promotion plan, sales plans, or this public offering statement once registered, without notifying the state Real Estate Commission. Then the developer must amend the public offering statement to include the changes approved.

We suggest that you take a look at the public offering statement given you by the developer of the condominium you are considering. Use items A through I above as a check list. You should find these and more in the public offering statement. If one or more are missing, ask the salesman for the information omitted. And be on your guard. Go over the public offering statement in detail with your lawyer.

2. *Purchase agreement* or *contract to buy*. When you've decided to buy and are satisfied with the price and terms,

you'll have to sign a purchase agreement or contract that specifies what you're willing to pay and what the seller is willing to deliver. This is a legal document and must be written according to the provisions of the laws of the state. Among the important points you'll want to examine:

A. It should disclose fully all the facts about the project.

B. If it does not, it should tell what document does and where, when, and how you may see it. Most states require that the buyer be offered this public offering statement, prospectus, or "disclosure document" before the sale can be made. The buyer often must sign a statement certifying that this document has been given to him to read, and specifying the date he has received it.

C. The contract should state what other documents about the project exist, such as (1) the declaration, (2) by-laws, (3) survey and plan.

D. What arrangements are indicated if the developer does not sell enough units? (1) Can you cancel? (2) Can you move in and rent? (3) If you move in as a renter, can you apply all or part of your rent money to purchase of the unit? (4) What happens to your deposit money in this event? Is it applied toward rent? Specifically prevented from use in construction? Automatically returned to you? Be sure to find out.

The essential elements of a condominium purchase agreement or contract are these:

A. Description of the specific unit, address, and legal name and location of the project. This paragraph may include information about the overall project, the units that are part of it, their prices, their individual portions of the overall assessments, voting rights in the association, and down payment required for each unit.

B. Price you've agreed to pay and the method of payment, i.e., how much down upon signing the purchase agreement and how much at some later date(s) and how much at the closing.

C. Deposit. The seller should agree (in writing) that the

deposit and any money received before the closing will be placed in an escrow account at a bank with interest credited to you. It should state that the seller may not receive any of the escrow money until the deed is conveyed to you, the buyer. Deposits should be returnable to you during the cooling-off period, upon request.

D. Conveying title. In this paragraph the seller will state how and when free and clear title to the unit will be conveyed to the buyer. It may state specifically when, or it may (if the project is incomplete) call for the buyer to pay the balance due within a certain number of days (thirty days, for instance) after the seller notifies him that the unit is ready to be turned over. This paragraph will also spell out what closing costs the buyer may expect to pay and which ones (if any) the seller is going to pay. (In an FHA purchase agreement this paragraph includes that agency's official estimate of the market value of the unit.)

E. The homeowners' association (HOA) arrangements should be outlined, and your voting power as owner of this specific unit should be stated. The paragraph may simply say that the association will operate and maintain common areas and facilities, that each owner will be a member and subject to the by-laws and regulations of the association.

F. Cancellation rights should be stated. Among these will be death of the buyer and default in payments. Some contracts permit the buyer to be released if he finds another purchaser suitable to the seller. Some contracts are conditional on buyer's creditworthiness. In other words, if the seller finds that you can't get the mortgage money he may decide to cancel and return your deposit (usually keeping a portion as compensation for his time and trouble).

If the seller fails to deliver or convey title free and clear on or before the specified date given in the contract, the agreement can be canceled and the buyer's down payment is to be returned.

The intent of this paragraph is to ensure timely delivery so that you are not kept waiting for months beyond the stated delivery date. That can be very costly. Just think what it means when you sell your present house on April 30, expecting to move into your new condominium home per schedule on May 1, but cannot. You have to live somewhere, and that means either breaking your contract to sell your house or finding temporary accommodations until the condominium is ready for occupancy. One schoolteacher we know moved from her apartment in August when her lease expired, expecting to be in her condominium home for the beginning of the school year. Her unit was not complete. She was forced to live day to day in a nearby hotel or cancel her condominium contract. It was mid-November before she was able to move in. She could have canceled if she had wished. And you should have this option also. Make sure it's in the contract.

G. Cooling-off period. This should be written into the contract. It gives the buyer a chance to change his mind within a specified time period, usually from five days (FHA-approved contracts) to ten days (Virginia condominium law). More than that, it gives you time to go over the documents in detail with your lawyer, banker, and/or accountant. Virginia's law gives buyers ten days from date of signing the contract or receipt of the public offering statement (prospectus or disclosure document), whichever is later. If the seller is notified in writing within the cooling-off period that the buyer wants out, the seller must return his money and the agreement is canceled. No reason need be specified.

Read this clause carefully—if it's in the contract at all—for it may have some verbal curves or loopholes in it.

H. Attachments. Frequently the contract will call for the official certified documents to be attached. These should include the declaration, by-laws, management agreement, survey, and plans, each an important, fundamental document that you should read and understand thoroughly before you buy. The contract should list the attachments; check them off to make sure they are all included.

I. Budget. The developer's estimate of the annual and monthly costs of running the development and providing for contingencies should be laid out for you before you lay down any of your money or sign any papers. (See Section 4 in this chapter.)

3. *Declaration (also called conditions, covenants, and restrictions [CC & R], enabling declaration, and master deed).* Legally, the condominium is born only when the declaration, survey, and plans are recorded officially. It is the developer who files these papers that establish the condominium. That action changes the deed covering the previous property into a "common estate" consisting of a specified number of dwelling unit estates. The individual estate owners share the "common estate" deed—they have an "undivided interest" in it. All of the individual unit estates must be described within the total estate. Everything not specifically described is part of the common estate, owned jointly by the individual estate owners. (This includes land and structural elements such as roofs, the space between units, etc.)

The declaration contains a legal description of the boundaries of the entire property. It also must specify the boundaries of the individual units. Since words are clumsy in such three-dimensional situations, the survey and plan are necessary to show where the buildings are located on the property and where the respective units are located in the buildings. Streets, parking areas, and recreation facilities will be described in the declaration and shown in the survey and plan.

It is in the declaration description and survey drawings of the condominium that you will learn whether any part of the project has been reserved by the developer. If you don't find it out now by carefully going over these two essential documents, you will surely find out when the first month's assessment comes due.

The declaration is a cornerstone of the whole condominium structure. It sets down on paper many fundamentals. Here, for instance, you will find the proportion of your unit to the total number of units in the project for voting and assessment purposes. Since that vital figure determines your monthly payments, taxes, and voting power, it is extremely important to you. The point may be made in the declaration as to how this percentage may be changed. In most declarations this proportion cannot be changed (nor can any part of the declaration) without unanimous consent of the homeowners.

RED FLAG: If your declaration reads otherwise, be sure to question it. Have your lawyer review it for sure. It may be that the developer has written in a clause that allows him to change your proportion without unanimous consent of the owners—in which case your vote against the matter may be overridden.

In the declaration you will find out where your "estate" stops and "common areas" begin. This spellout may be similar to this description that appears in the Virginia condominium law:

To the extent that walls, floors and/or ceilings are designated as the boundaries of the units or of any specified units, all doors and windows therein, and all lath, wallboard, plasterboard, plaster, paneling tiles, wallpaper, paint, finished flooring, and any other materials constituting any part of the finished surfaces thereof, shall be deemed a part of such units, while all other portions of such walls, floors, and/or ceilings shall be deemed a part of the common elements.

If any chutes, flues, ducts, conduits, wires, bearing walls, bearing columns, or any other apparatus lies partially within and partially outside of the designated boundaries of a unit, any portions thereof serving only that unit shall be deemed a part of that unit, while any portions thereof serving more than one unit or any portion of the common elements shall be deemed a part of the common elements.

Subject to the [previous paragraph], all space, interior partitions and other fixtures and improvements within the boundaries of a unit shall be deemed a part of that unit.

Any shutters, awnings, window boxes, doorsteps, porches, balconies, patios and any other apparatus designed to serve a single unit, but located outside the boundaries thereof, shall be deemed a limited common element appertaining to that unit exclusively.

In this description it should be clear that the common area begins behind the wallboard or plaster, between finished flooring and underfloor, and above ceiling tiles and between them and beams or joists. Window glass and doors are part of your unit also. The sewer pipes are yours until they join with those of at least one other unit, as are pipes, conduits, chutes, flues, and so on.

Many have been the arguments in condominium HOAs over what is and is not the common area, and therefore to be maintained by the owners' association. That is why declarations and state laws now define this matter with some care. Note that in the Virginia law limited common elements are enumerated with more than the usual precision. This is because limited common elements are the responsibility of the individual owner, usually, even though he does not have title to them. In other words, they are for the exclusive enjoyment of his unit and its residents, but, though he will have to keep them clean, painted, and repaired, he will never own them outright.

What about common elements? What happens if a pipe breaks in the wall between your unit and your neighbor's? A clause in the declaration usually will state that the common or "party wall" should be repaired at the joint expense of adjacent owners, unless one of them is guilty of negligence which caused the problem.

Owners, under the declaration, may not sue for partition

of the common areas. This means simply that you can't stake out your 200 square feet of yard and plant a tomato garden. Or anything else not approved by the HOA or the board of directors. Owners also agree, in accepting the declaration, as to what restrictions, if any, are to be placed on them. Among others, usually, is a prohibition on business or trade uses of the unit (including garage or other structures) by the owner, tenants, or guests.

Generally the declaration prohibits owners from renting their units for transient or hotel purposes—defined as any period less than thirty days or rentals in which the occupants receive customary hotel services such as maids, bellboys, and room service. However, units may be leased for longer periods, subject to tenants' abiding by the same rules, regulations, and covenants as owners.

The declaration should state what kind of insurance coverage will be carried and under what plan damaged property will be disposed of or repaired.

What if you want to maintain or bring into your unit underground lines (water, TV, electric, heat, steam, sewerage)? The declaration will probably state that it must be done by the agent(s) of the HOA, subject to the deed and declaration and other documents, such as the by-laws. The purpose here is (a) to prevent do-it-yourself buffs from doing an inadequate job that will endanger or diminish the property of others in the development, and (b) to prevent owners from getting the idea that they can duck or reduce their monthly assessments for maintenance by "taking care of their own." (In a Woodside, California, condominium, townhouse owners dug into the hillsides under their units to make storage rooms. This could have endangered building foundations, for the earth under some units was too unstable for this kind of operation.)

The declaration may establish control over the recreation facilities, defining what they consist of and who may use them. Typically, all owners and their resident families are entitled to use the pool, tennis courts, etc. Each unit is obliged to pay a specified percentage of the annual costs for insurance, reserve for replacement, maintenance, and operation of the facility.

Sometimes recreation facilities are established as a corporation separate from the condominium. It will then have a membership, board of directors, and officers of its own. In any case, whether for a roof or a tennis court, the capital expenditures needed for major repairs or capital improvements generally will require the O.K. of two-thirds or more of the unit owners.

RED FLAG: The lease. What's the danger? The developer may retain title to vital sections of the project, such as the swimming pool or parking areas, tennis courts, gymnasiums, recreation rooms, etc. If you've bought your unit believing that you had wide-open access to any or all of these features, it will come as a costly jab in the pocketbook when you're asked to ante up.

But that's only the beginning. You're likely to find that you have no control whatever over the fees charged for use of any of these leased facilities. That means they will be priced at whatever the landlord can get from you and your fellow owners. New York State, California, and the FHA do not allow such leases. As condominium expert Professor Patrick Rohan of St. John's University notes, owners of such condominiums have really been buying the tail and getting stuck with the dog. "I know one builder," he says, "who could have given his condominium units away for all the money he is making on the leases."

Leases are common in Florida condominiums. You'll find that you cannot refuse to pay for the rental of leased facilities even if you don't use them. The developers have anticipated this. In your Florida deed you'll find a clause that states in no uncertain terms that your refusal or failure to pay can result in a lien on your unit. And if you still don't pay, the leaseholder can press for foreclosure of your mortgage. As the old vaudevillian used to say, "Some of the best clubs get you by the [prices on] drinks." Condominium leaseholders get you by the pool, parking space, tennis, and other recreation rents. (In 1973, 20,000 Floridians petitioned their state legislature to ban ninety-nine-year recreation leases. In 1974 the Florida legislature took a giant step, passing legislation that will make it possible for buyers of new condominiums to buy up the leases applying to their projects—after ten years. Buyers before 1974 are stuck.)

It is because of such elements as leases in the declaration that you need a skilled lawyer's help—preferably one with condominium experience. Consider, for example, the experience of David W. Unterberg.

A lawyer who was senior enforcement officer of the Securities and Exchange Commission's New York office in the 1940s, Unterberg headed his own law firm in New York in the fifties. By 1971 he was comfortably well off and decided to retire and move to Florida. He found an attractive condominium in a 650-unit high-rise project called Century 21 Admiral's Port in North Miami Beach. He bought.

It was when he claimed his covered parking space that he ran into trouble. He discovered that it was not included as part of his purchase, though he had been told it was in the package. The parking place, he learned, would cost an additional $1,000. This, the developer told him, was all perfectly clear in the title document (declaration). Yes, the 200-page declaration did mention parking spaces. But an amendment took away buyers' rights to them. Considering that the parking-space matter took up very few lines in the 200-page tome, it's not surprising that even an experienced lawyer such as Unterberg overlooked it. "Let's face it, I was conned," says Unterberg, referring to the hidden clauses and lying salesmen who hoodwinked him.

But Unterberg is a remarkable man. Not only was he

outraged when he discovered that he had been ripped off on his parking space; he did something about it. As a lawyer, he knew how to dig for information, how to follow through the legal channels, and, since he was retired, he had the time to bulldog the case.

Unterberg brought suit to acquire his promised parking space. The judge dismissed the case. Unterberg appealed. He lost. Determined to carry the matter further, Unterberg conducted a two-year investigation. The information he uncovered was startling and eventually brought to public attention the intricate background of the Century 21 project.

The development began in 1970 as a 6,600-unit condominium to be built on 160 acres in North Miami Beach. Construction and other costs ballooned fantastically beyond budget. Building dragged far behind schedule. Sales were miserable. By mid-1971 one of the financial backers considered declaring bankruptcy for the project. He took the alternative of peddling a block of twenty-nine units for $1 million to a group of New York investors. But these money men insisted on a return on their money, which meant that the original condominium declaration had to be amended so the twenty-nine units could be rented to the public. Among the amendments was one that took out the parking-space entitlement of Unterberg and his fellow condominium buyers.

It seems that the original developers had also bankrolled a wallboard installation corporation. They had a 50 percent interest in it. This corporation had a $1.1 million contract to do the interiors for the first 650 units of Century 21. As early as February 1971 the costs had more than doubled—to $2.4 million—and the work was still far behind. At that point the developers tried to cancel their contract with the dry-wall corporation—but workers continued to show up at the site, despite police and armed guards hired to keep them away.

Lawsuits between the developers and the other owners of the dry-wall company produced charges and countercharges. The developers claimed that the other faction in the dry-wall company had purposely boosted construction costs to "force and coerce" them to turn over ownership of the corporation.

The construction specialists charged that the developers had purposely ordered extra work and exorbitant practices (such as putting thirty men on a task that required only ten) in order to escalate the project's construction loan. Why? To funnel construction funds into their own pockets.

In court, neither side proved its case.

However, the facts reveal that the construction company's overrun cost each condominium owner more than $1,500. Furthermore, this particular ploy was only one of several. Century 21 had "sweetheart" contracts with seven companies that its developers had created to siphon off profits— companies involved in everything from basic construction to decorating the finished units, plus a 5 percent management contract and a lease for the recreation facilities (a pool and a polluted beach) running $20,000 a month at present. (In July 1974 the developers offered—for the sixth or seventh time—to settle all outstanding lawsuits brought by Century 21 unit owners. The offer, in part, called for cancellation of the management contract, $200,000 in cash, and the opportunity to buy up the recreation lease.)

At last report, Unterberg is still trying to get his covered parking space.

"What is sickening is to see how many ... people buy condominiums without hiring a lawyer," says New York's Assistant Attorney General David Clurman, a lawyer and a leading authority on condominiums. "People wouldn't dream of buying a single-family house without counsel. Getting a coop or condominium is more intricate." All of the conveyance, title, and mortgage work required in a conventional house purchase are needed plus analysis of the lengthy offering plan or declaration and additional research beyond that.

Consider how you might fare faced with two hundred

pages or more of legalese and real estate jargon. The point is that you should have a lawyer skilled in condominium practice. And if the property you're considering is out of state, it can, as Professor Patrick Rohan puts it, "contain dynamite." He warns: "If it does, and if you have an untrained lawyer or one who glosses over the plan or doesn't read it, then you are in real trouble."

What should you do? Professor Rohan recommends calling the bar association in the condominium's state. Ask to be referred to a lawyer qualified in condominium practice.

The declaration will state that each owner is automatically a member of the Homeowners' Association—HOA—(sometimes called the Unit Owners' Association or Council of Co-owners) during the time of his unit ownership. As such, he agrees that administration of the condominium will be in accord with the declaration and by-laws.

Here a statement is generally included that common expenses (i.e., monthly assessments) unpaid by any owner will constitute a lien on that owner's unit. This lien may be foreclosed by a lawsuit undertaken by the condominium manager and actually carried to the point of auction at a foreclosure sale.

RED FLAG: Look out for a clause in the declaration that gives the association first refusal rights to any sale of a unit. What this means is that when you decide to sell and have found a buyer, you must put the deal before the association. It may review it and nix the sale. It must then meet the price offered, but this may entail further negotiation on your part and may delay closing or kill your deal. Essentially, this kind of clause (known as a restraint on alienation) in the declaration means that you are not free to sell your unit as you should be with any property you own in fee simple. This kind of restriction is an open invitation to the exercise of prejudice and exclusionary whims. Such clauses are ruled out in some state condominium laws, such as Virginia's.

Search the declaration, your contract, deed, and all descriptions of the development for mention of any phase-type construction. It's a fast curve. If it's in the documents, it may give your developer the legal right to control the project for years, so long as construction continues, for instance.

RED FLAG: There are several dangers in this. He may boost the maintenance charges and other fees over the objection of unit owners, for instance. He also may build additional units whose owners and families will use the facilities you consider just adequate for your phase of the construction. You can readily see how your interest in and use of the common facilities of the condominium will be diluted if two hundred more families (for instance) are added to the project.

The developer may argue that your share of maintenance charges will be reduced by the addition of scores (hundreds?) of new unit owners. Be skeptical. (Phrasing such as this is outlawed in strong state condominium laws.)

Another seemingly innocuous clause that can handicap you and your co-owners if you have to file a lawsuit against the developer may be in the declaration. Look for a paragraph stipulating that no financial resources of the HOA can be used to hire an attorney to contest the developer's general plan of development.

RED FLAG: The plan of development, filed with the original condominium declaration by the developer, may specify his intention to enlarge the project with additional phases. (That's why it's important to see the whole declaration.) It may, in fact, give him wide latitude in enlarging the project—far beyond his verbal or printed statements about keeping the project to a certain size.

The declaration should include a clause stating that the seller will be subject to the declaration, by-laws, and other documents that apply to buyers and that he will take no action that will adversely affect the HOA or prevent it from pressing to have defects or oversights in construction fixed.

RED FLAG: Look out for devices the developer may use to control the condominium. Among these: clauses in the declaration that benefit him to the detriment of unit owners.

Example: The developer may buy or keep one or more units of the condominium. Remember that the declaration setting up the project requires unanimous approval in order to change it. Thus the developer, by owning at least one unit, may block changes by casting a "no" vote even after he has turned over to the HOA the running of the project. Some state condominium laws require that the developer state how many, if any, of the units he intends to own and/or rent out. If you don't find any information on this in the documents, ask.

Under Virginia's condominium law the state real estate commission must investigate after a developer files a condominium registration application. This investigation makes a number of valuable examinations that help protect a prospective condominium buyer. For example, the commission:

A. Determines whether the developer can really sell the units he's offering if the buyer complies with the contract (i.e., does or will the developer own them, according to the legal documents?).

B. Looks for "reasonable assurance" that all the proposed building and improvements will be completed (i.e., does the developer have the money and know-how?).

C. Reviews the advertising materials and promotion plan. These must be truthful and comply with the commission's rules, affording full and fair disclosure.

D. Checks to see whether the developer or officers and principals of the development corporation have criminal records or citations for false or misleading promotion schemes involving land or condominium sales either in the United States or abroad.

E. Makes sure that the developer has complied with Virginia laws covering condominium sales offers.

For an inkling of how valuable this Virginia condominium law is on these vital points alone (not to mention its great value on myriad other points), just ask yourself how you would attempt to secure the information and evaluate it accurately on any one of these five fundamental matters. Prospective condominium buyers will be better served when there is a federal law giving strong protection of this sort or equally penetrating state laws on the books across the land.

The Virginia law has a particularly significant clause that really expresses the heart of it. In a section dealing with the developer's control of the project and how he may phase out, the law winds up with this statement: "This section shall be strictly construed to protect the rights of the unit owners."

You'll have to search a long way to find that straightforward a position in real estate ordinances and legal papers elsewhere.

4. *Budget.* The salesman should be prepared to sit down with you and detail the estimated annual and monthly assessments for maintenance, rubbish removal, reserve assessments, taxes, and insurance for the entire development and for each specific unit, such as yours.

This information is due you before closing. Insist upon it.

The earlier you have it, the better. And don't let the salesman tell you the developer doesn't have such figures or can't get them. That's bilge. He's supposed to be a professional in the real estate field and is in a far better position than you to estimate such cost factors and project them over a time frame of a year or more. (Some management services, using sophisticated computer models, project costs for periods of eight years.)

It's true that budgeting is difficult, especially because costs are so volatile. Yet in many cases developers are selling units mainly on the basis of their attractive prices. As they say, "It ain't only the cost, it's the upkeep" you must know to make an intelligent purchase.

For the developer, setting out such a budget may be risky. If he understates the figures by a wide margin, he may be liable to lawsuits for fraud by purchasers and to prosecution for violation of condominium laws in states that try to protect consumers against "low-balling."

You know what low-balling is—you meet it in its most virulent form on used-car lots. There the salesman will quote a low, bargain price on a car. You snap it up. As you sign the contract, the salesman just happens to remember: the vehicle has new snow tires and a new battery—and a new price. It will cost you $50 more than he quoted. If you take it, you've been taken. That's the price he had in mind all along; the first one was a phony—he "low-balled" you.

It's not a simple matter to determine whether a developer has deliberately low-balled in his advertising and selling of a condominium. At Farm Hill Vista, a 150-unit condominium at Woodside, California, the original market price was $35,000 for three-bedroom, two-bath units in 1973. After five months of full-scale operation the monthly fees and assessments package had to be raised $8 to $10 per unit. A year later these monthly charges totaled around $48 for that basic unit. But its market value had jumped to $42,000.

Do residents blame the developer for the vaulting monthly

charges? No. According to George Burger, former president of Farm Hill Vista Association, the increases are "due to double-digit inflation and things like three gas and electric rate hikes in one year."

In the case of Kimberly Place at Wheaton, Maryland, units originally sold for $30,000 to $35,000 in 1972. The developer made two mistakes in stating that monthly operating fees would be a flat $14 per unit. His first blunder was to underestimate costs so the entire budget projection was low. His second mistake? He ignored Maryland's condominium laws, which state that such costs must be prorated according to each buyer's percentage of ownership. Result: In mid-1974 monthly assessments ranged from $25.09 to $34.75 per unit.

As George Burger points out, "Assessments should be presented in a more realistic light. Regardless of how accurate the developer's estimate is, the buyer must be made to understand that costs are bound to go up. They're sure not about to go down."

To illustrate how condominium budget figures are developed and can be laid out, here is an example.

The development consists of fifty-two two-story, three-bedroom, two-and-a-half-bath townhouses known as Mililani Garden Homes, Unit 1. It is located on the island of Oahu about eighteen miles from the center of Honolulu. The project includes an eighteen-hole championship golf course and a two-acre recreation center with community building, Olympic-size pool, locker rooms, meeting rooms, and so on.

Each unit has living area of 1,282 square feet, lanais and balconies of 120 square feet, carport of 177 square feet, and a site totaling 1,600 square feet. The fifty-two units are on 4.6 acres, for a density of eleven units per acre. (Moderate density.) Four of the units are larger and are priced at $40,200 each; the remaining forty-eight units are priced at $33,900 each.

DEVELOPER'S
BREAKDOWN OF PROJECT EXPENSES

House Construction	$904,800	
Paving, Utilities, etc.	48,000	
Trash Facilities	4,000	
Survey and Stakeout	1,500	
Maps and Prints	1,200	
Landscaping and Irrigation	18,000	
Loan Commitment Fee	19,152	
Construction Bond	9,000	
General Excise Tax	9,000	$1,014,652
Architectural & Engineering	$ 41,200	
Advertising & Promotion	15,000	
Sales Commissions	18,200	
Legal Fee	3,000	
Appraisal Fee	2,000	
Closing Costs	5,200	$ 84,600
Construction and Incidental Expenses		$1,099,252
Land and Site Improvements to Date	$398,156	
Service Fee at Delivery (2 points)	25,536	
Interest	27,757	$ 451,449
TOTAL PROJECT COSTS		$1,550,701

OWNERS' ESTIMATED COMMON EXPENSES

	Budget for 52 Units	
	Monthly	Annually
REQUIRED FUNDS:		
Operating Expenses @ $34.84/month	$1,811.56	$21,738.72
Community Association Dues @ $5.25/month	273.00	3,276.00
CATV @ $6.24/month	324.48	3,893.76
TOTAL @ $46.33/MONTH	$2,409.04	$28,908.48

BREAKDOWN OF OPERATING
  EXPENSES:

Administrative @ $5.00/month	$ 260.00	$ 3,120.00
Workmen's Compensation @ $.98/month	50.96	611.52
Insurance, Fire, Liability @ $5.20/month	270.40	3,244.80
Repair & Maintenance Reserve @ $11.85/month	616.20	7,394.40
Utilities: Common Area Electricity @ $1.50/month	78.00	936.00
Common Area Water @ $3.00/month	156.00	1,872.00
Salaries & Wages	260.00	3,120.00
Supplies & Tools	20.00	240.00
Other Expenses	100.00	1,200.00
	$1,811.56	$21,738.72

Real estate taxes in Hawaii are calculated on 70 percent of market value of the property. The assessment is $20 per $1,000 valuation.

ESTIMATED TAX CALCULATION

70% × $34,000	=	$23,800
$20/$1,000 × $23,800	=	476 per year
Monthly tax payment (476/12)	=	39.68/month

(Hawaii has a home exemption for those who qualify. It would deduct $8,000 from the assessed valuation and lower the taxes on this unit to $316 a year.)

Putting these elements together gives us the figures for:

MONTHLY PAYMENT ANALYSIS

Sales price: $34,000
First mortgage of 90% for 29 years @ 7½% interest
Mortgage amount: $30,600

Mortgage monthly payments	$215.30
Maintenance fee	29.64
Real estate tax	39.68
Mortgage insurance co. premium @ ¼% for 9 years	6.38
TOTAL:	$291.00

Note that the intrest rate stated in this example is only 7.5 percent—far below the going rate at this writing.

What income would you need to qualify for a mortgage on this condominium unit? The banks in Hawaii generally work on a 4 to 1 ratio. That is, your monthly gross income (not including overtime) should be four times the amount of your housing costs, in this case, 4 × $291 = $1,164, or an annual income of $13,968 or better.

(This example was prepared by Wendell Brooks, Jr., CPM, vice-president of Mililani Town, Inc., and past president of the Hawaii Association of Real Estate Boards. It is presented here with his permission.)

5. *Survey and Plans.* Don't confuse this with the drawing of the project in the sales literature. This is an official document, registered with the municipality.

Though the condominium laws of the various states differ, each is concerned with title and therefore requires a precise picture of the property to be bought/sold and recorded. The phrase "cubes of title" is often used to indicate that for condominiums, unlike land transactions, you are dealing with a three-dimensional property.

Generally the survey and plans will include:

A. A survey of building location "as built," drawn to

American Land Title Association standards. It should indicate the boundaries of the project, locate each building relative to the boundaries, show all recorded easements, exceptions, and rights of way, indicate elevation above sea level. All setback and/or building restrictions should be shown. The survey is important for the future because it should locate sewer, water, gas, electric, and TV lines and pipes.

B. Plans of each building in the project, giving floor-by-floor layouts, with specifications and relative locations, should be supplied. Each unit will have a number identifying it in the building, just as each lot in a subdivision has its own specific number.

C. Elevations or vertical renderings are required. These drawings are especially important to show the locations of units in high-rise buildings. They give the third dimension to the condominium survey documents, showing where in space the specific units are to be found, and because of this, they are essential.

The plans must be certified by a surveyor, engineer, or architect, as required by the laws of the state. If these elements are complete, titles to the units should be relatively easy to establish and transfer without serious complications.

6. *By-laws.* As many real estate experts see it, a condominium's by-laws actually are a constitution for a mini-government, a "condomocracy." By the provisions of the by-laws the homeowners' association (HOA) is created and the duties, obligations, and powers of its officers and board of directors are delineated. Furthermore, the by-laws guide and govern the mutual relations between the many families who live together in the condominium project.

Dr. Carl Norcross, in his study *Townhouses and Condominiums,* puts it this way:

An association is a little democracy, run like a New England town meeting. But the day-to-day problems of self-government are probably far more difficult to solve wisely than were faced by small New England towns. A large number of strangers are thrown together who must sort themselves out, choose their leaders, and start managing a complex operation in a very short time.

If you were moving to another country, you'd want to know before you went as much as possible about it—especially such basic factors as its government, tax structure, services to its people, opportunities, and restrictions. You'd want to know so you could evaluate what your life would be like there. You'd probably not want to go to a dictatorship, or a place where taxes are high and always advancing. Nor would you choose a place where roads, schools, hospitals, sanitation, fire and police protection are poor, where you could not pursue your basic interests because of various prohibitions or shortages.

Think about those points as you read about "another country" you may be moving to, the condominium you're considering. If it's still unfinished, the by-laws may give you an essential peek at how it will shape up after the colonists have landed.

The key elements of the by-laws are these:

A. Self-government—setting up the homeowners' association that will run the community. This part of the by-laws will set out the regulations for holding meetings, election of officers and directors, their powers and responsibilities, quorums, voting, and the mechanics of running the association.

B. Phase-out of developer control—this section should specify the responsibilities of the developer to start and/or support the HOA and specify when and how his control of the HOA will end. (See discussion in the section on the declaration.)

C. Operations and upkeep—this section should spell out owners' liabilities, rules, regulations, and resolutions governing the community (comparable to ordinances in municipal government), and such important matters as maintenance, assessments, expenses, and reserve provisions.

D. Insurance.

E. Special provisions.

The developer writes the by-laws and files them with the state authorities at the same time he registers the declaration and survey. The developer usually administers the condominium until the first annual meeting of the HOA, at which time the board of directors and officers may be elected from among the owners and take over management of the project. (The by-laws for small projects may not require boards or officers.) The first part of the by-laws, therefore, usually will state who qualifies to be a member of the HOA, how votes are determined, what the board of directors will consist of and how its members are elected, how the officers are elected and the powers and responsibilities of these representatives of the unit owners. Even the impeachment procedure should be included, in case the HOA members want to throw out a director or officer for some legitimate reason.

The technical paragraphs about quorums, proxies, special meetings, methods of voting, and so on are dry reading but of primary importance. One of the major surprises of the ULI survey was the degree of resentment, discouragement, and disillusion that many residents felt about their associations. But it is the association that is fundamental to the operation of a condominium. Joint ownership of common areas—grounds, recreation features, parking—and maintenance of the property are the major attractions of condominium life. And where an HOA either on its own or through hired managers runs an attractive, efficient condominium, the property values are likely to reflect this, with better-than-average appreciation in value.

No one should underestimate the complexity of HOA responsibilities in a condomocracy. A new condominium is like a compressed instant village, with roads, recreation, painting, parking, cleaning and club activities, cup-of-sugar neighborliness and no-no naughtiness in a population explosion from zero to several hundred people of sundry types and ages. No wonder some HOAs have stormy times. No wonder they are often seriously misunderstood. One resident complains, "It's just too socialistic for me." Another, equally unhappy, says, "Our association is a dictatorship."

"Emphasize to prospective owners," advises a real estate man who owns a condominium, "that an efficient association is a combined responsibility, not a matter just for the board." His plea, if heeded, would have prevented the unfortunate reaction of one government worker–condominium owner who growls, "I felt total disgust for the sales people and all the 'yes' people in the builder's office—people who don't deliver on promises of what the association is supposed to do. I'm not getting services I was promised and I don't like paying for something I don't get, or for paying somebody to tell me what I can do with my own property. . . ."

Obviously there was a considerable communications gap between this buyer, the developer, and the association directors. If he had been aware of the seldom-mentioned restrictions and responsibilities as well as the highly touted advantages of condominium life, he would either have passed up this purchase or been better prepared for what he encountered. More and more developers have come to understand that they have a duty not only to start the HOA and set it on course, but to help train and guide its directors, officers, and membership in self-government. If the association is hamstrung by quarreling, the condominium project will suffer and with it the developer's reputation, his investment, and his future sales.

So the phase-out of developer control of the HOA is extremely important. It is often (the temptation is to say invariably) a period—after owners have moved in and before they have taken over control—racked with tensions, stresses, and strains. The owners generally suspect the developer's motives, resist his actions, and press to end his influence as quickly as possible. The developer wishes to maintain control of the project until his investment matures—that is, until all the units are sold. And the provisions of state laws frequently dictate the limits to developer control and participation in the HOA.

In the by-laws you should find a time schedule specifying when the developer must relinquish control of the HOA. Usually there are at least two possibilities: whichever comes first, the sale of a specified percentage of units (60 percent, for instance) or after a specified time (two years, for example). The new Virginia law puts these figures at 75 percent and two years, respectively.

RED FLAG: Often the developer is sufficiently interested in maintaining an attractive appearance for his project until most if not all units are sold that he will absorb some of the maintenance costs or carry out substantial maintenance activities at his own expense. However, the developer, in the declaration or by-laws, may attempt to push off on purchasers his own share of the condominium common area and recreation facility maintenance costs. The language may vary, but here is the detour to watch out for: After the first ten (say) of the project's fifty units have been sold, the maintenance fees for the entire project are assessed to this group of ten owners. The developer steps aside. What happens? The unlucky ten are hit with maintenance charges two and a half times what they should be, until the rest of the units sell. But it could be even worse.

Example: In one excruciating case, $2 million worth of recreation facilities had been built for a two-thousand-unit project. But sales lagged and only three hundred families moved in. They could not carry the costs intended to be spread over two thousand families. The developer couldn't or wouldn't make up the difference. The mortgage on the recreational facilities was foreclosed.

Among the ways in which the developer may exercise control over the project before it is finally turned over to the HOA, one favorite is veto power. He extends to owners and their association various elements of decision-making, but he retains the final word.

Example: The by-laws call for the HOA to process all applications for architectural changes—but the developer has the final approval.

Example: By-laws call for the HOA to prepare the project operating and capital budgets—but the developer has the right of review, amendment, and rejection of line items.

Example: Selection of the managing company or agent is up to the HOA—but only with the O.K. of the developer.

One extremely important provision of the Virginia condominium law voids all contracts and leases entered into while the developer is in control of the HOA, unless the owners ratify them when they take control. Thus the state's law makes it impossible for a developer to ram down the throats of unit purchasers any fifty-year "sweetheart" maintenance contracts (for example) without the express vote of the owners when they take over the HOA.

Example: One Florida developer signed a twenty-five-year management contract with a fledgling company at a time when he still controlled the condominium association with more than 51 percent of the votes. Dissatisfied members of the board of directors looked into this and discovered that one of the owners of the management company was (guess who?) the developer.

Builder's warranty—Virginia's new second-generation condominium law requires that the by-laws contain certain provisions and suggests others. Among the required provisions is a warranty against structural defects. This warranty covering individual units must extend for one year from the date you receive title. And for common elements of the project it must extend one year or until 60 percent of the HOA votes have been transferred by the builder to the purchaser, whichever is latest.

RED FLAG: If the law in your state does not require this type of warranty statement, ask the developer what he will guarantee. He should spell out (a) the time span over which he will guarantee his construction, and (b) what the warranty covers.

Into each life some rain must fall, and in each building project some callbacks are inevitable. What are callbacks? Warranty situations in which you must call back the contractor to take care of loose ends and construction problems that crop up after everything seemingly was completed. Wise developers provide for callbacks by including an increment of about 3 percent of overall project costs as a set-aside for just this purpose.

The three Rs—rules, regulations, and resolutions—can be dynamite. Sometimes unpopular or unreasonable rules are passed at a meeting of the HOA. There are cases on record where irate residents have sued the HOA successfully, claiming they were denied due process.

One method of decreasing misunderstandings and the resulting friction is to put together a "book of resolutions." This may include policy resolutions designed to help the HOA run its affairs. This "book" sometimes is drawn up by the developer before the HOA comes into being, or by developer and owners before turnover of control to the owners. Of course the HOA can amend or throw out any or all of the resolutions, but at least it has a framework of operations with which to start.

Example: Lack of rules and regulations can bring about crisis situations. At Farm Hill Vista condominiums in Woodside, California, there were no rules for use of the swimming pool during the first summer. The HOA's former president, George Burger, remembers: "Without any rules, people went swimming with long hair and no bathing caps and with layers of suntan lotion. The pool equipment just couldn't take it. (The filtration system was so overburdened that maintenance had to be done five times a week instead of two.) We had to sit down virtually in a state of crisis, write a complete set of swimming-pool rules, and then try to enforce them."

Sometimes the rules are carried to absurd lengths. We know of a high-rise condominium on Long Island where the rules are twenty-three pages long. Titled "A Brief Summary of the Unit Owner's Guide to Congenial Living," there are pages and pages of nit-picking detail, of which the most confusing is this contradictory injunction: "All terraces must be kept free and clear of snow, ice, and any accumulation of water. Dirt and snow may not be thrown or swept off the terrace." It also orders that all animals must be kept on leashes, including birds and reptiles!

Some veteran condominium owners heatedly condemn the "life of ease" advertising used to sell condominiums. They contend that a realistic set of rules and regs and a mandatory reading of them by each new buyer would solve many problems.

"It's misleading," emphasizes Butch Kaufmann, manager (and a unit owner) of Los Gatos Woods, a 240-unit development in Los Gatos, California, "to tell people to 'forget your lawn mower and live a life of ease.' The developer should emphasize the C C and Rs (covenants, codes, and restrictions).

He should make it clear that everyone will be subject to these rules—the parking restrictions, the speed laws, the pet controls, the rule against running a business in your garage. A lot of buyers never read the C C and Rs, so they're shocked when someone comes around with a citation for an infringement. That's unfair to the people who do read the rules and move in thinking it will be a nice way to live."

It is the condominium's "rulebook"—those rules and regulations set down by developer and owners—that determines the day-to-day life of the project. This can be amended or modified as the HOA members desire, by formal vote. It is these rules and regs that put a curfew on use of the pool, or restrictions on hi-fi volume, hours of music practice, parking by visitors, and pet roaming. In other words, the public/social/recreational life of the condominium community is largely defined by these by-laws.

The by-laws should be drawn up in such a way that they give the HOA broad powers. Among these may be to:

A. Make improvements or additions to common elements.

B. Hire or fire agents and employees.

C. Grant or withhold approval of any change in the exterior of any unit or portion of the condominium by any owner. (This often is exercised through a committee on architectural control.) The architectural control function is an important one. Its purpose is to set guidelines for the exteriors, landscaping, and recreational and common facilities. The guidelines often are included in the original by-laws and modified by the HOA through amendment and addition.

In general, the architectural control committee is supposed to keep the exteriors "harmonious," as described in the agreed-upon guidelines. So if owners begin painting their doors and trim nonapproved colors, the architectural control committee issues a no-no. Changes in exteriors must first be approved by the ACC.

Example: Approval may even be required in the case of a

safety hazard. Balconies at Farm Hill Vista in Woodside, California, had dangerously wide gaps between railing slats. Owners insisted on adding slats to prevent children and pets from falling. The ACC issued specifications for the material to be used, its dimensions, and color of stain. The board of directors made it formal.

Obviously such minute restrictions concerning the facades of the project are not pleasing to every resident. In fact, they exasperate some people beyond endurance. "The association wants to exert its influence merely for the sake of exerting itself," fumes one unit owner, a chemical engineer, in the ULI study. "It is useless in getting something done, like improving the parking situation. They are more concerned about what color you paint your door, and whether you put your garbage out front or out back. They try to control what a person does with his own private home. When we terraced our lawn, which was impossible to mow because of steepness, they wanted to submit our idea to the vote of all homeowners."

Yet this owner and most others would agree that they were attracted by the appearance of the entire project and would admit the link between appearance and market value.

Generally the better state condominium laws require a clause in the by-laws about upkeep of the condominiums. Virginia's new law keeps it brief, simply says powers and responsibilities for maintenance, repair, renovation, restoration, and replacement of the condominium belong to the association in the case of common elements and to the individual unit owners in the case of any unit, its parts, and limited common elements.

Typically an owner is obliged to repair promptly anything in his own unit and his limited common elements which if not done would affect the entire project or other owners. He is expressly responsible for damages and liabilities he may cause or which may result from his inaction. An owner must reimburse the HOA for expenses in repairing or replacing any common area facility damaged by him.

The by-laws will state the owners' obligations to pay fees and assessments levied by the HOA. These are intended to cover:

A. Maintenance and upkeep.

B. Management fees and salaries.

C. Reserves—deposits for operating contingencies and capital replacements.

Don't look for any specific dollar figures in the by-laws. Costs change too fast for that. However, the developer should have given you an estimated budget for the project along with the contract and public offering statement. As we have noted, such budgets are estimates, at best, and may be far off target. You can imagine how difficult it is to project a budget for an unbuilt multiple-dwelling project several years into the future. Most of us can't project our own family expenses two months ahead.

Another element that may throw a projected budget out of whack is one that is impossible to predict: the level of expectations of owner-residents. Community management expert David B. Wolfe says he never has seen a budget analysis where the maintenance fees were related to standards of service. In other words, how often is the grass cut, fertilized, and watered? How often is the hallway carpeting vacuumed? Shampooed? Replaced? How often is the parking area resealed? By what specifications? And how often is it resurfaced?

"Even an adequate projection can be thrown off," he notes, "if the residents' level of service expectations is higher than originally presumed." (See the discussion of budget earlier in this chapter.)

There seems to be little or no relationship between original unit cost and monthly assessments. In the ULI study of 1,760 families in 49 developments there was no discernible pattern. Here are figures on assessments in some of the most expensive and least expensive condominiums, in both East and West. Also, the lowest and highest fees are noted.

Name of Development	Price Range (in $1,000s)	Monthly Assessment
Washington, D.C., area:		
Tarlton	$20–27	$ 4 (lowest fee)
Prospect Walk II	32–36	4 (lowest fee)
Habitat I	22–27	35 (highest fee)
Worland	69–86	10–20
California area:		
Creekside	17–25	5 (lowest fee)
California Villa Estates	21.3+	10
Sandpiper, Indian Wells	53–60	100 (highest fee)
Deane Homes, Big Canyon	64–145	100

It should be noted that in general the eastern condominiums in the study were older than those in California. Still, there is no evident correlation between price and age.

The by-laws generally specify that the board of directors may establish reserve requirements and assess owners for them. It comes as a rude shock to many new owners to discover that in addition to maintenance and operating fees there are fees for reserves with labels such as "general operating" and "common element (or capital) replacements." The shock would be eliminated if developers supplied a schedule of building reserves in which the expected life of common structural and mechanical elements was specified. Thus a built-up roof would be listed for replacement in twelve years, carpeting in five, and so on. Such a schedule, if supplied, is an indication of a thorough, conscientious approach on the part of the developer. Here, for different types of condominium construction, are the reserves estimated by one condominium expert:

RESERVE REQUIREMENTS PER MONTH
(as a % of Monthly Assessments)

	Capital/Replacement	*Operating*
Townhouse, brick	10%–15%	3%–5%
Townhouse, frame	12%–18%	3%–5%
Garden apartments	6%– 9%	3%–5%
Elevator apartments	3%– 6%	3%–5%

Note that operating reserves are about the same proportion of monthly assessments, regardless of type of construction. However, if you are seeking economical living with minimum costs, the monthly reserve assessments for elevator apartment condominium capital reserves are as little as one-fifth of townhouse capital reserves. The reasons are fairly obvious in the two vastly different types of building and grounds. The area of roof per unit in the high-rise condominiums, for instance, is a tiny fraction of the roof area per townhouse unit. Ditto landscape (generally), gardens, and so on.

The FHA recommends that the general operating fund be built up to at least 15 percent of the total of annual assessments. It also requires its mortgagees to keep such reserves in special safe accounts such as insured bank accounts, or invested in U.S. government-guaranteed obligations. (In 1973 an IRS ruling, #74-17, stated that condominium associations are not tax-exempt. Therefore their reserves are considered taxable "profits" by the IRS. Legislation to change this inequitable ruling is expected to clear Congress in 1975.)

The operating reserve is supposed to "provide a measure of financial stability during periods of special stress and may be used to meet deficiencies from time to time," according to the FHA. It may be useful to remember that the FHA limits disbursements from the general operating reserve to 20 percent of the balance in the fund at the end of the previous year.

RED FLAG: Are reserves really important? Only if you expect to live in the condominium more than three or four years after it's built.

"Go down to Florida, where the high-rise condominiums are," explodes Charles A. Goldstein, a New York lawyer specializing in condominium law. "I dare you to find a building that has a contingency fund at all, let alone one that is adequate for major structural improvements."

So what?

"So, of course, what will happen is this: Repairs will be made on a catch-as-catch-can basis. But when it makes sense to replace something, it will be patched up instead. So what we now have in these high-rise condominiums is built-in early obsolescence." In a sense, builder and buyers are both gambling that expensive replacements won't be required before they are out of the picture—removed from the scene by sale of their interests or, especially in the case of retired elderly buyers, by something even more final, death.

Example: Imagine that after eight years the roof of the building goes bad. There is no reserve to replace it. You (and the HOA) have to go to all the unit owners and ask them to approve a special assessment of several hundred dollars apiece. You knock on the door of a man seventy-eight years old who has been paying on his condominium for eight years. He has limited income, a limited future, and because of these conditions a limited outlook. He's not inclined to increase his monthly expenses. It may be extremely difficult at that late date to secure the necessary money from all the owners. Or even to get them to approve a special assessment in the HOA meeting if many of them also are elderly and retired.

Real estate specialists complain that even where condominium reserve accounts have been established, their bases are often questionable. Usually they are simply a percentage of total assessments (as we have illustrated above), not the result of careful, estimated-life audits of major components. Yet the most businesslike approach to reserve assessments surely is to work from an inventory of common area facilities/ equipment through an estimated-life audit to establish a reasonable annual reserve requirement for replacement of the inevitable wearouts.

The initial insurance policy when new owners move into the project will have been taken out by the developer. It is one of the first items the directors of the HOA will wish to review. The coverage should include:

A. A master casualty policy insuring against fire and other hazards plus vandalism, malicious mischief, windstorm, water damage, boiler explosion, etc. Coverage should be for 100 percent replacement value, minus foundation excavation and land values (these items will survive almost any mishap). Building service equipment should be included. Experts recommend an "agreed amount" endorsement and a "condominium replacement cost" endorsement.

B. A "legal expense indemnity" policy will protect the HOA officers and directors from lawsuits and claims stemming from their association duties.

C. A master public liability policy with a severability of interest endorsement, covering the HOA, officers and directors, managing agents and/or employees plus all unit owners and others (such as tenants).

D. Other required policies, such as workmen's compensation, vehicle liability, and special coverage on land or improvements, etc., including the recreation facilities.

E. The policies should be cancelable or modifiable only after prior written notice to all owners/members of the HOA.

In summary, by-laws are not so hard and fast as the declaration. They can be changed by vote of the association membership—usually a simple majority of those present and voting. The by-laws will spell this out as part of the mechanics of doing business—meeting calls, quorums, amendments, voting, and proxies.

By-law amendments may be fundamental. At Kimberly Place, a 174-unit condominium in Wheaton, Maryland, in two years the amendments included one indemnifying officers and directors against lawsuits; one allowing unscheduled emergency board meetings; and one giving HOA members more than one proxy vote and allowing proxies to be counted in a quorum. (These proxy provisions were necessary because so few owners came out for meetings.)

The Virginia law suggests that a quorum consist of 33 percent of association members, theorizing that you're not likely to get much better participation from people who have bought into a project because they're after "carefree living." This quorum figure is stated in the by-laws from the first, but may be changed by vote of the membership at any time.

7. *Boards and committees.* The board of directors of the HOA is really its executive council. But it is limited in size, expertise, and amount of time its members can devote to running the affairs of the development.

Sometimes it is limited in other ways. A townhouse owner who is a real estate economist complains in the ULI study, "Our association charges the board with establishing suitable rules for use of facilities, but no authority to discipline offenders. . . . We have had fine neighbors forced out of the community by thoughtless neighbors. They violate the rules so fast the board can't keep up with them. . . ."

Typically, most condominiums have committees for major problem areas such as:

A. Finance—charged with riding herd on budgets of other committees and all accounting and budgeting matters of the HOA and its hired management, including general operating budget and periodic financial reports.

B. Grounds—this one monitors and supervises landscape maintenance.

C. Recreation—designed to supervise and schedule use of recreation facilities and plan activities.

D. Architectural control—to pass on changes or modifications of all exterior and interior common areas and such responsibilities as the HOA may decide (see earlier discussion in this chapter). At some condominiums this committee also receives bids for repainting and other routine building maintenance.

E. Grievances—or, if you prefer, community relations. This one obviously can be crucially important. It may operate as the liaison between board and complaining owners in developments where there is no manager and the board deals with complaints. In the larger projects it may screen complaints, settling the minor ones before passing the others along.

In the community relations committee at Los Gatos Woods there are six subcommittees. Each has a major area of concern: recreation, grounds, youth, publications, special projects, and parking and traffic. (This last can be a hot assignment. Many studies confirm that parking problems are one of the most-cited complaints of condominium residents.)

You shouldn't be deceived: It takes time and effort to serve on a committee. Most HOA directors find themselves putting in as much as ten hours a week on HOA business. And committee members may easily put in dozens of hours if and when their committee is involved in a special, knotty problem.

RED FLAG: The fact of having committees is no automatic answer. One unit owner who is an engineering consultant laments in the ULI survey, "I'm an officer of our maintenance committee. There are four others on the committee, all intelligent, concerned men, but innocent and naive when it comes to running this operation. Why can't someone ... set up and run a seminar for townhouse officials to aid them in making proper decisions on lawn care, winter problems, architectural control, and other problems?"

One way of tackling this is to bring together into a handbook the organizational manual and operating procedures for the HOA. This handbook then is distributed to all board and committee members and committee chairmen. Community management expert David B. Wolfe recommends that this handbook should include:

A. An introduction to the condominium concept, defining it, its purposes, and a brief history.

B. Physical description of what the condominium owns and manages.

C. An organizational description of the condominium with the legal documents that created it.

D. A cross-index of all legal documents that apply to the condominium—municipal, county, state, and federal—so directors can quickly refer to specific legal requirements or authority for action.

E. General operating procedures, including model fiscal controls, financial procedures, outline, meeting agenda, plus a description of service delivery methods, the scope of board activities, responsibilities of board officers, and the purposes of policy resolutions.

F. Job descriptions for HOA employees, their salary ranges, benefits, model employment contracts, and the like.

G. A committee system for performing much of the HOA work. Criteria for committees, their function and scope, responsibilities of ad hoc and standing committees, and operating guidelines for specific committees should be spelled out.

H. Maintenance specifications to guide the association in negotiating contracts and in assessing the performance of the managing agent.

I. Models of various administrative forms needed to run

the condominium, such as proxies, nominating petitions, policy resolutions, rules for the pool, applications for architectural control review, and so on.

J. Sources of additional information such as consultants, government agencies, professional organizations, etc.

It should surprise no one that preparing such a handbook and distributing it does not end problems and confusion. It is usually advisable to augment and reinforce what the handbook spells out. One useful avenue for this, and an excellent channel for intracondominium as well as developer/owner communication, is a periodic newsletter. Distributed to all housing units in the condominium, it can carry topical news as well as interpretive and factual treatments of the handbook provisions, the by-laws and rules and regs and their application to residents.

Not so incidentally, especially if you become a board member, it can be vitally important to indemnify the board and HOA officers against lawsuits and damage claims.

Example: In an Illinois condominium the board continually ignored complaints about roof leaks from a number of senior citizen resident/owners. The board thought they were simply cranks. But when a severe spring rain struck, the leaky roof collapsed. There was water damage to the units, their furnishings, and owners' possessions. Personal effects insurance claims by several unit owners were paid promptly by their insurance companies. But the companies instituted suits against the board for these losses, claiming the board was liable because it did not carry out its duties—it did not make timely repairs.

8. *Management agreement.* "The problem with our homeowners' association," snorts one unit owner, "is that everyone has his own ideas about how it should be run. My opinion is that you should hire a consulting firm when you

become too large to be arguing over fence colors or problems with a lifeguard who offends one owner at the pool."

Most sizable condominium projects with problems like these take a different route. They hire a manager or a management company.

A condominium manager's life—to paraphrase Gilbert and Sullivan—is not a happy one.

How could it be, with as many would-be bosses as there are adults in the project? If he's lucky, he may average only one cataclysmic problem per week from each unit. Not to mention the ongoing duties such as maintenance, cleaning, grounds keeping, and riding herd on pets, children, flora, fauna, and visiting relatives and deliverymen. Certainly presenting ever-higher bills for necessary goods and services wins him no kudos. But how could it be otherwise in these inflationary times?

In short, you may pity the poor condominium manager, but after all, it's a free country and he chose his work.

RED FLAG: Often the developer hires a manager or management company before the owners take over the HOA. This first manager is inevitably suspect. Owners look upon him as the developer's agent rather than theirs. New, first-time condoleers expect the entire project to be letter-perfect from the word go—and they hold the manager responsible for that unattainable perfection. As costs and assessments escalate during the first-year operations, the manager is the conspicuous, convenient target for blame. Furthermore, the manager is the man in the middle, between the directors and the owners, carrying out directors' orders.

Is a manager necessary? Not in smaller condominiums, if you can get owners to take over management duties on a voluntary basis. But be realistic: The response you're going to hear again and again is "Look, I pay thirty-five dollars a month for someone else to do this for me and I don't want to be involved."

There's another angle to consider: "Having been on our board for two years," says an owner who is a secretary, replying to the ULI survey, "I know one of the greatest needs is better property management companies. Also, if board members do not have management experience it can be disastrous." Not everybody has management experience sufficient to run a condominium.

How small—or big—must a condominium project be to have (or need) professional management? That's one of those nigh-impossible questions. A simple project with no recreation facilities, few common areas, and 100 or even 200 units and enthusiastic, knowledgeable owner participation might do very well without professional management. In contrast, a seventy-five-unit project with marina, tennis, pool, and highly demanding, busy owners might well require a staff and sizable budget.

The management agreement should state several things to make sure both manager and residents understand what is expected. To begin with, the manager is hired by the association through its board of directors, and it is to the board that he reports. He counsels with the board and receives instructions from it. The manager hires staff according to job descriptions, operating schedule, and wages approved by the HOA. He is responsible for the efficient functioning of the staff.

The manager and staff are confined, so far as their duties are concerned, to the common and recreational areas and facilities of the condominium, unless otherwise directed by the HOA. (For instance, in case of a vacancy for which a rental is required, the manager might put the unit in shape and act as rental agent.)

Here are typical manager responsibilities:

A. Receive, record, and act upon requests and complaints of unit owners.

B. See to it that owners perform the maintenance they are responsible for. (In some projects owners clean and care for the yards in front of their units, for example.)

C. Collect monthly fees and assessments from owners and renters. Keep accounts showing income, delinquencies, expenditures, reserves, deposits.

D. Maintain the buildings, grounds, and facilities, including cleaning, painting, decorating, plumbing, carpentry, and other repair work, up to a maximum cost per item or repair as specified by the HOA.

E. As directed by the HOA, take out necessary insurance.

F. Act as paymaster for wages, insurance premiums, bills, collections, reserve deposits, taxes, and government assessments.

G. Maintain office records, books, and accounts subject to examination by the HOA or its agents at all reasonable hours; render monthly and annual reports with the aid of an accountant.

How much and on what basis is the manager to be paid? Some contracts call for him to receive a fee as a percentage of his gross collections; others are on a straight salary basis.

Note that there is a fundamental difference between the objectives of a condominium manager and those of a rental apartment manager. In the condominium complex the manager works for and represents the owners directly, and his purpose is to serve them and preserve and protect their investments in their units and the property they own jointly.

In a rental project he works for the landlord and his goal is to maximize profits through the process of cutting expenses to the bone. Anyone who has lived in an apartment house where paring all but essentials was the landlord's method of squeezing the utmost out of rents will recognize the difference in objectives and the resultant quality of life.

RED FLAG: The management agreement should spell out the bases for terminating—allowing the manager to give notice and the HOA to fire the manager if either is dissatisfied. There is a danger in contracts that extend without cancellation clauses for several years. Such contracts can be a trap.

Example: Point East condominium in North Miami Beach had a twenty-five-year management agreement with an agent and an attorney chosen by the developer. So dissatisfied were the unit owners that their association went to court to break the contract. The state supreme court upheld the agreement and the HOA now prefers to pay out $60,000 annually to the managing agent and $10,000 to the lawyer just to keep them *off* the property! In addition, the HOA has filed an antitrust suit, charging that the contract was a "tie-in" in restraint of trade.

The developer says, "The courts have held that all of the contracts and documents are valid. Everything was there for them or their attorneys to read well before they bought their apartments. There has never been any question of fraud or the misuse of funds." (Maybe the question is one of buyer illiteracy on a mass scale.)

This may be a downbeat way to wind up this chapter and this book. But the example could not be more appropriate in underlining the importance of professional help in your condominium quest. Rely on your banker, accountant, or tax adviser, and by all means on a real estate lawyer. Their fees will be worthwhile in saving you much grief, in avoiding pitfalls, and in launching you safely on a new way of life in your condominium.

Glossary

APPRAISAL An evaluation of the property to determine its value (which usually means its market value).

ARCHITECTURAL CONTROL BOARD Committee of the HOA which passes on any changes to the exterior of the condominium unit.

AS-BUILT DRAWINGS Drawings that show what actually was installed: sewer lines, electrical conduits, etc.

ASSESSMENT *Operating* assessment means proportionate share of the budgeted annual cost of maintaining the common areas and elements of a condominium and sufficient reserves to assure financial stability. The annual assessment is reduced to monthly charges payable to the HOA. *Special* assessment is for special purpose or to cover inadequate budgeting of operating expenses.

BINDER Money paid to secure the right to purchase real estate upon agreed terms.

BOARD OF DIRECTORS Homeowner members of the HOA elected by the HOA to run or to hire a management team to run the development.

BY-LAWS The constitution and working rules of the con-domocracy, written and filed by the developer, along with the declaration or master deed.

CC&R See Declaration.

CERTIFICATE OF TITLE The paper that signifies ownership of a unit.

CLOSING The date on which title for property passes from the seller to the buyer and/or the date on which the borrower signs the mortgage.

CLOSING COSTS Costs to complete the purchase over and above the price of the unit. They include mortgage service charge, title search, insurance, and transfer of ownership charges (paid each time the unit is resold or refinanced).

CLUSTER A grouping of low-rise housing units to ensure maximum open space around the units.

COMMON AREAS OR COMMON ELEMENTS Those parts of a condominium not specifically delineated or privately owned, but owned jointly by all unit owners.

CONDOLEER One who lives in or owns a condominium unit.

CONDOMANIA Rapid spread of condominiums.

CONDOMINIUM Individual ownership of a dwelling unit and an undivided interest in the common areas and elements that serve the multiunit project.

CONDOMINIUM ASSOCIATION See HOA.

CONDOMOCRACY Self-government of the condominium by the HOA.

CONTRACT Purchase agreement, *legally binding*.

CONVERSION Turning a multiunit dwelling from rental form to condominium form.

CONVEY To transfer title from one person to another.

COOPERATIVE A multiunit dwelling in which residents own stock, but not their individual units, and operate and manage the dwelling for their common good.

COVENANT A promise usually in the form of a recorded agreement when used as a part of real estate language.

CUBES OF TITLE Drawings and description of a condominium as a three-dimensional property.

DECLARATION A document that contains conditions, covenants, and restrictions governing the sale, ownership, use, and disposition of a property within the framework of applicable state condominium laws.

DEED A document that is proof of ownership of your individual unit and common elements.

DENSITY Number of housing units per acre.

EQUITY The value of a property, less mortgage and other debts. Buyer's equity increases every time a monthly mortgage payment is made.

ESCROW Money or documents held by a neutral third party until all conditions of a contract are fulfilled.

FHA Federal Housing Administration of the Department of Housing and Urban Development.

HIGH-RISE Multiunit dwelling more than four stories high (what we think of as an apartment house).

HOA Homeowners' Association. An organization consisting of *all* condominium unit owners, which is established for the purpose of running the development.

HUD Department of Housing and Urban Development.

LEASE Document allowing for the use of property without purchase, in return for stipulated payment(s).

LIEN A claim recorded against a property as security for payment of a just debt.

LIMITED COMMON ELEMENTS Those elements that are attached to individual units, such as shutters, window boxes, patios.

LOW-BALLING Low quotation, purposely given or not, by salesman of costs of housing unit, taxes, fees, and other charges relating to purchase.

LOW-RISE One- to four-story multiunit dwelling.

MAINTENANCE FEE Cost of upkeep and repairs of common elements and facilities in a condominium development.

MASTER DEED see Declaration.

MORTGAGE A lien on real property that an owner gives a lender as security for repayment of the borrowed money.

MORTGAGEE The homeowner who is obligated to repay the mortgage loan on the property he has purchased.

MORTGAGE INSURANCE Provided by FHA or a private company for a fee. It makes possible lower down payment on a mortgage and repays lender in case of default.

MORTGAGOR The lender who has advanced money to the mortgagee.

OILSR Office of Interstate Land Sales Registration of HUD.

PHASE CONSTRUCTION Development planned in phases.

Builder completes one phase before beginning construction on the next.

PHASE-OUT Time at which developer relinquishes his control of project.

POINTS (Also called mortgage discount.) An inducement by the buyer and/or seller to entice lender into making the necessary loan. One point = 1 percent of the amount of the loan. If the loan is $20,000, one point is $200. If lender says points are expected to be paid on the loan, shop around for a better loan.

PROSPECTUS Official, legal explanation about development and developer as filed with state or other government authorities.

PUBLIC OFFERING STATEMENT See Prospectus.

PURCHASE AGREEMENT See Contract.

RESERVES Funds that are accumulated on a monthly basis to provide a cushion of capital to be used for contingencies. There are general operating reserves and replacement reserves (used to replace common elements such as roofs as needed at some future time).

SEC Securities and Exchange Commission.

STATUTE A law passed by a legislative body and then set forth in a formal document.

SURVEY Official determination of the lot lines, dimensions, and legal locations of property to see what precise perimeters of the property are and to see if there are any existing easements or encroachments.

THREE RS Rules, regulations, and resolutions are the by-laws under which the HOA functions. See By-laws.

TITLE Evidence of a person's legal right to the possession of property, usually in the form of a deed.

TITLE INSURANCE Special insurance to protect lenders or purchasers against loss of their interest in property due to legal flaws in title.

TITLE SEARCH Examination of courthouse records to determine whether title to the property you are buying is free and clear, unencumbered by liens, assessments, ownership disputes, restrictive covenants, or other claims that would jeopardize your legal right to the property.

TOWN CLERK The office of a local community where real estate transactions are officially registered.

TOWNHOUSE One- to four-story attached or semiattached housing unit.

UNDIVIDED INTEREST In condominium law, this applies to the joint ownership of common areas not owned individually.

VA Veterans Administration.

WARRANTY In condominium law this generally pertains to builder's guarantee against structural defects. Guarantee usually extends for one year from date title is passed.

ZONING Regulations passed by locality to restrict or limit type of building that can be done in a particular area or zone and to restrict uses of the property within a specified zone.

ZONING BOARD Body of local officials who pass the regulations that restrict property and land use.

Check List of
Closing Documents

As a check list of elements to be supplied at or before the closing, the FHA "Required Closing Instruments" list is useful. Here are some of the key items (among other technical items) in addition to the deed and mortgage:

1. Evidence of zoning compliance by the builder.

2. Certificate of occupancy from the municipality.

3. Escrow deposit agreement (FHA has a suggested form for this, #2456).°

4. Surety bond against latent defects (FHA #3259) ° or evidence of an escrow deposit by the builder in the amount of 2 to 3 percent of the total mortgage amount. This is the deposit that helps pay for construction flaws—leaky roof, crumbling sidewalk, faulty wiring, etc.

5. Escrow agreement for off-site facilities (FHA #2446),° which covers any deposit you may make toward a swimming pool or golf course, for instance.

6. Master deed or enabling declaration (FHA #3276 or 3276-A).°

7. By-laws of the condominium (FHA #3277).°

8. Regulatory agreement (FHA #3278).°

9. Purchase agreement (FHA #3279).°

10. Survey or condominium plat drawing.

11. Management agreement (FHA #3281) ° for professional operation of the condominium.

° We have mentioned here the numbers of the FHA forms for these documents. We strongly recommend that you secure copies of these from your local banker or FHA office. If they cannot furnish them, write directly to Federal Housing Administration, Department of Housing and Urban Development, 451 7th Street, S.W., Washington, D.C. One publication contains them all. It is *HUD Handbook 4265.1, Home Mortgage Insurance—Condominium Units, Section 234(c)*.

The official FHA forms are helpful because they show what the federal government recommends that these vital documents contain in order to protect you, the buyer. The information in these forms gives you bench marks against which to compare the documents supplied by developers and other sellers.

Bibliography

USEFUL BOOKS AND PAMPHLETS:

Clurman, David, and Hebard, Edna L. *Condominiums and Cooperatives.* New York: Wiley-Interscience, 1970.

Department of Housing and Urban Development, Washington, D.C.:

—*Condominiums, Their Development and Management,* by Anthony D. Grezzo, 1972.

—*Mortgage Insurance Handbook for Condominium Housing Insured Under Section 234(d) of the National Housing Act;* Circular 4580.1; June 14, 1973.

—*Home Mortgage Insurance—Condominium Units Section 234(c);* Circular 4265.1; July 30, 1973.

—*Questions About Condominiums,* June 1974.

—*Wise Home Buying,* November 1972.

Florida Condominium Directory. Tampa: Trend Publications, published biennially.

Kass, Benny L. *Homebuyers Checklist.* National Homebuyers and Homeowners Association, 1225 19th St., N.W., Washington, D.C. 20036.

Norcross, Dr. Carl. *Townhouses and Condominiums: Residents' Likes and Dislikes,* Urban Land Institute, 1200 18th Street, N.W., Washington, D.C., 20036, 1973.

Securities and Exchange Commission. *Condominiums Registered Under the Securities Act of 1933.* Economic Staff Paper 74, no. 1, July 1974.

PERIODICALS:

The Condominium Report, newsletter published monthly by Warren, Gorham & Lamont, Inc., 89 Beach Street, Boston, Mass. 02111.

Condominium World, magazine published by Warren, Gorham & Lamont, Inc.

House and Home, magazine published monthly by McGraw-Hill Book Co., New York, N.Y.

NAHB Journal-Scope, publication of National Association of Home Builders, 15th & M Streets, N.W., Washington, D.C. 20005. Carries "Best Housing Awards" each October.

PUD Review, newsletter published monthly by Community Management Corporation, 1831 Michael Faraday Drive, Reston, Va. 22090. (PUD stands for "planned unit development.")

Index